COMMANDO

THE AUTOBIOGRAPHY OF JOHNNY RAMONE

WRITTEN
BY

Johnny Ramone

EDITED BY **JOHN CAFIERO**
WITH **STEVE MILLER** AND **HENRY ROLLINS**

For Abrams:
Designer: Jacob Covey
Production Manager: Jacquie Poirier
Managing Editor: David Blatty

Ramone, Johnny, 1948–2004.
  Commando : the autobiography of Johnny Ramone / by Johnny Ramone.
  p. cm.
  Includes bibliographical references and index.
  ISBN 978-0-8109-9660-1 (alk. paper)
  1. Ramone, Johnny, 1948–2004. 2. Punk rock musicians—United
  States—Biography. 3. Ramones (Musical group) I. Title.
  ML419.R324A3 2011
  782.42166092—dc22
  [B]
                2010032482

"Today Your Love, Tomorrow the World" written by Dee Dee Ramone,
Johnny Ramone, Joey Ramone and Tommy Ramone, © 1976 (renewed),
WB Music Corp. (ASCAP), Taco Tunes (ASCAP) and Evergreen
Entertainment Group Inc (ASCAP). Lyrics reprinted by permission.

"Wart Hog" written by Dee Dee Ramone and Johnny Ramone © 1984 ·
Taco Tunes (ASCAP). Lyrics reprinted by permission.

Published in 2012 by Abrams Image, an imprint of ABRAMS. All
rights reserved. No portion of this book may be reproduced, stored
in a retrieval system, or transmitted in any form or by any means,
mechanical, electronic, photocopying, or otherwise, without written
permission from the publisher.

Printed and bound in China
10 9 8 7 6 5 4 3 2

Abrams Image books are available at special discounts when purchased
in quantity for premiums and promotions as well as fundraising or
educational use. Special editions can also be created to specification. For
details, contact specialmarkets@abramsbooks.com or the address below.

THE ART OF BOOKS SINCE 1949
115 West 18th Street
New York, NY 10011
www.abramsbooks.com

www.johnnyramone.com

IT'S GREAT TO READ JOHNNY RAMONE'S STORY IN HIS OWN WORDS. It's like having a personal audience with him. It has his pacing, his timing, his rhythm. It's a nice fast read—just the way he would have wanted it.

I always liked Johnny. He was smart and entertaining and fun to be with. I first met him in the high school cafeteria at a table where he was holding court. He was the center of attention—something he had to be. A friend introduced us, and that was it. For the rest of the year I would sit at his table. What I really liked about Johnny was his sense of humor. He was sharp as a tack and loved to outsmart you. In fact, he loved to outdo you in any endeavor—he was the most competitive person I ever met.

In those early years, what bonded us was music. The Beatles had just hit our shores a few months before, and there was a mad passion for all the pop bands that were sprouting up. Soon we had our own band, called the Tangerine Puppets. Johnny was an amazing showman in that band. He would hold his guitar high like he was carrying a machine gun and move ferociously on the stage like he was possessed, flinging himself wildly around and undulating with the rhythm. He was the essence of rock and roll.

Johnny was meant to be a musical warrior. Joey, Dee Dee, and I gravitated to him because he was so charismatic and interesting. He was the magnet that pulled us together. In this book, Johnny talks about the hard road traveled through his personal and musical life. It is an insightful and interesting story indeed.

—*Tommy Ramone*

I WAS THE KING OF THE HILL WHEN I WAS ONSTAGE. THE RAMONES TOPPLED THE MOUNTAIN.

It was that power of the guitar: I walked out there knowing that we were the best. There was nobody even close. Volume was my friend and I never wore earplugs. That would have been cheating.

After retirement came induction into the Rock and Roll Hall of Fame, victory in readers' polls that surveyed influential bands, and even me getting ranked as the sixteenth top guitar player in history by *Rolling Stone*.

But for all the success, I carried around fury and intensity during my career. I had an image, and that image was anger. I was the one who was scowling, downcast, and I tried to make sure I looked like that when I was getting my picture taken. The Ramones were what I was, and so I was that person so many people saw on that stage.

That was both the real me and the image me who beat up Malcolm McLaren in the tiny backstage area at the Whisky a Go Go in Los Angeles in 1978. The place is a great club on the west end of Sunset Boulevard that holds about three hundred people. It has a history of great music, from the Doors to the Stooges to the New York Dolls.

McLaren was talking to my girlfriend, and all of a sudden I decided I didn't want her talking to him anymore, so I told her to come over to where I was standing a few feet away. I heard McLaren ask her, "What's his problem?" So I went over to him and said, "What's my problem?" and I punched him in the head. He went down but I wasn't done. I went over and grabbed Dee Dee's bass to finish the job, but people intervened and hustled McLaren out of there.

The rage started with adolescence and never fully left. I would walk off the stage with that anger going, although it eased when I retired in 1996. While retirement seemed to soften me, the prostate cancer I was diagnosed with in 1997 did so even more. It changed me, and I don't know that I like how. It has softened me up, and I like the old me better. I don't even have the energy to be angry. It has sapped my confidence. I fought it as hard as I could. I figured it would win in the end, but I hate losing. Always did. I liked being angry. It energized me and made me feel strong.

When I was younger, I was ready to go off at any time. My wife, Linda, and I would go out to the Limelight in New York, and I would see people and be able to freeze them with a look. People were even too scared of me to tell me that people were

"THE RAMONES WERE FUN,
AND THE MORE INTENSE, THE BETTER.
OUR SHOWS HAD VIOLENCE."

scared of me. I could tell that some people were just uncomfortable around me. I never tried to make that happen; it just did.

I really never felt out of control. It was just the way I lived my life. I was the neighborhood bully.

I even beat up Joey, our singer, one time, before we were in the band, back in the old neighborhood. He was late to meet me—so I punched him. I was twenty-one; he was nineteen. We were meeting up to go to a movie. There was no excuse for being late.

Once we did start playing in the band, we had fights like any gang of guys. Even onstage at the very beginning, we fought over what songs to play. We'd yell at each other, "Fuck you," you know. Then walk offstage, come back and play some more. At CBGB's especially, we'd start a song and an amp would malfunction, and we'd all have to stop. We'd already be excited to play, and then have to stop, so someone would yell, usually Dee Dee, "What the fuck is wrong?" Then someone else would yell back at him to shut up. And on it went. It was an extension of what happened in rehearsal. We forced ourselves out of it when we decided we just wanted to play the songs quickly.

When we started touring, I had to smack Dee Dee a couple of times to get him into the van after stopping for gas at a roadside stop. One time I smacked him outside the Tropicana Hotel in Hollywood. He was high on something, as usual. I liked him, really, but I think he just liked to be difficult.

Marky, our second drummer, and I would go months without talking to each other over some stupid thing, like who should sign what. We were in Japan, and he had a cracked cymbal. I thought we should all sign it and sell it. He and I actually had a fight over whether the band should sign it or just him. He thought that since he was the drummer, he should be the one. I thought a fan would rather it be signed by the whole band than just Mark. We all ended up signing it and selling it.

With Joey, I'd try to like him, talk to him, then it just went bad. He was a fucking pain in the ass. So I gave up.

The reality is that I was surrounded by these dysfunctional people, and I was the one who ran the business end, aside from our managers. Everybody else was a mess—in their own world pretty much. We traveled by van, and someone would want to stop every fifteen minutes. So I had to tell them that we could only stop every couple of hours. Otherwise we would never have gotten to any shows.

The Ramones hinged on aggression, and balanced that with the cartoon-like fun that so many people seemed to see in us. So the anger was diffused in the public eye a lot of the time.

I was so bent on making us the best band in the world, I was willing to do anything without compromising us.

The first time we played CBGB's, Alan Vega from Suicide came up and told us that we were the band he'd been waiting for and he couldn't believe how great we were. I told Dee Dee, "Look, we fooled someone. Maybe we can fool other people."

Every time we had a new fan in those early days, I'd say, "Fooled another one." Then I realized at some point that we really were good.

But what people saw had deep roots, even though it was pure rock and roll. What we did was take out everything that we didn't like about rock and roll and use the rest, so there would be no blues influence, no long guitar solos, nothing that would get in the way of the songs.

The Ramones were fun, and the more intense, the better. Our shows had violence. We had fights; we had blood. I'd have been bored crazy if crazy stuff didn't happen.

At one point in the early nineties, I came into possession of a canister of police-issue mace, compliments of a former New York City cop. In fact, he was with us working as part of the crew at this show in Washington, D.C. It was a sturdy can, big enough that your whole hand went around the canister, not one of those little things that women carry. I figured he knew how to handle the mace, so I told him to get ready and fire it into the crowd at some point during the show.

So he got behind a PA column and let go. It was terrific, like a bomb went off, with everybody running and pouring beer on their faces. That was a Ramones show.

CHAPTER 1

IT WAS THE NAMELESS GUY WHO CHANGED THE JUKEBOX RECORDS AT MY PARENTS' BAR WHO REALLY TURNED ME ON TO ROCK AND ROLL WHEN I WAS SEVEN YEARS OLD.

Jerry Lee Lewis, Elvis Presley, and Fats Domino. He gave me the singles he was taking out as he put in the newest hits. I loved it; I had a great collection of 45s. I still love that era of music. The songs sound so clear and exciting, like Little Richard's "Keep a Knockin'."

The bar was in Stewart Manor, which is a two-thousand-person population town on Long Island in New York mostly full of Irish immigrants and their descendants. It was a beer-and-shot joint with a great jukebox. My parents worked together and closed the place every Saturday. I stayed at home alone until two or three in the morning, from the age of seven to thirteen from 1956 to 1961.

But it was great having the place in the family. I would walk home from school and hang out there and listen to that jukebox full of powerful songs, stuff I had never thought existed. Sometimes my dad let me help him, and I would go downstairs to sort the bottles and put them in cases. I'd pass it on the way home from school in the afternoon and stop in; if a ball game was on, I'd stay and watch it. I'd hang out at the bar as much as I could.

My parents, Frank and Estelle, were working class all the way. My dad was full-blooded Irish, and my mom was Polish-Ukrainian. Both of my dad's parents

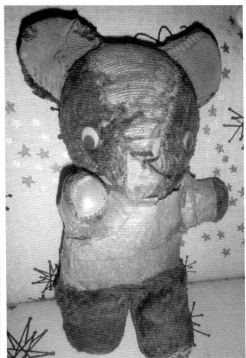

were born in the United States and deceased by the time he was a little kid. My grandparents on my mom's side were born out of the country. Her mother was born in Poland, and her father was born in the Ukraine. He died when I was twelve.

We were also Catholics, and I made my first Communion when I was six, but I quit going to church soon after that. I'd ask, "How come Pop doesn't go to church on Sunday?" And he'd say, "Well, I don't have to go." So I said, "Well, I'm not going anymore unless you're going." As with so many kids, I didn't do too well with the nuns, who would smack me around all the time. I don't think I even did anything to deserve it, but they would hit me with a stick. I got out of going to church school after I showed my mom the marks. I told her I wasn't going anymore. She didn't believe they were hitting me until I showed those to her. I'm still Catholic, I just don't go to church.

Soon after the jukebox guy started giving me those singles, I saw Elvis Presley on the black-and-white television

PREVIOUS: Johnny's first Communion. Photo used courtesy JRA LLC photo archives. All rights reserved.

OPPOSITE: Early photos of Johnny with his parents and with Santa, 1950. Used courtesy JRA LLC photo archives. All rights reserved.

ABOVE: Johnny, age four, August 1953, with the teddy bear still in his collection. Bear photo by Suzanne Cafiero.

in our Westbury living room, on *The Ed Sullivan Show*. The first time was September 9, 1956, in a broadcast from Hollywood; then seven weeks later from thirty miles away in New York City, at the CBS studio at Broadway and Fifty-third Street. Today that's the Ed Sullivan Theater, where Letterman does his show.

I just knew that I would be a big Elvis fan from that moment on. It was that wildness, and it really upset my parents, who thought he was a dope fiend. I didn't know what that was, but I figured it must be a good thing, because if it upset the grown-ups, it had to be good. I just followed him from then on and became a rock and roll fan forever, and by the next year I was listening to Ricky Nelson, the Everly Brothers, and was a big Jerry Lee Lewis fan. And Little Richard, I mean, he was gay and black, and that made everybody crazy. I'd probably like Pat Boone now, but back then, that was what parents listened to, which meant it was no way to really outrage them. That was one of the cool things about that music, how it pissed off the grown-ups. I would say I had the seed of rebellion very early.

It was easy to be a kid back then. All this good music was played on the radio, not like now. I would hear all of the greatest artists, Ricky Nelson, the Platters. I'd come home from school and watch *American Bandstand* at four P.M.

Westbury was half black when we lived

there, but it was a different country then, where everybody got along—you know, the 1950s. As an only child, I was by myself a lot, and we moved around, sort of climbing the economic ladder. We moved from Westbury to Stewart Manor in 1956 and stayed there for about five years. After that we moved to Franklin Square on Long Island, then to Jackson Heights in Queens until we finally moved to Forest Hills, another Queens neighborhood, around 1964. That was a new apartment building in a decent neighborhood close to the high school. It was considered an upper-middle-class area. My world was very small. I basically didn't leave my block or two.

So I went to a bunch of different schools, had to adjust a lot to new people. It was probably good for me, but I didn't like having to keep moving away from whatever friend or friends I might have made.

All of my fondest memories of childhood have to do with my father. He was a hard-drinking Irish guy who everyone liked. Our family had all our meals together when I was little. It was a real family. My dad for some time worked at Grumman, an airplane factory. He would come home from work and pull me out of bed and walk around the neighborhood with me on his shoulders, sometimes in the middle of the night if he was working a double shift. And he would have a beer after work and give me a sip when I was five or six. It tasted so good out of the can.

OPPOSITE: Johnny with his pop, age three, Christmas 1951.

ABOVE: "I've liked animals all my life. I always had pets when I was a kid, but they always seemed to disappear. I even took my pet poodle on the road with us in 1980. I've always enjoyed going to zoos." Both courtesy JRA LLC photo archives. All rights reserved.

In terms of time, I remember everything from my childhood by the year of baseball cards. I remember the first cards I saw were '54 Topps cards, a nickel a pack, which was wax paper, and they came with a stale slab of gum. Sometimes, even now, thinking about the cards takes me back to opening the pack in my neighborhood as a kid. That feels good, thinking of that. I remember standing behind my apartment building and opening a pack of 1957 cards. The first card I saw was a Raul Sanchez, from the Cincinnati Reds.

Baseball is the way I mark a lot of early things. Even the way I began to rebel had to do with baseball.

In 1960, I was sitting in my seventh-grade classroom during the Yankees-Pirates World Series, last game, and I had my transistor radio held up to my ear, listening to the game, and my teacher asked me what I was doing. I told her that I was listening to the World Series and that this was very important and that it was something that everyone should be listening to. She told me to shut it off, but I told her I thought we should put it to a vote and see who wanted to listen to the series. She just told me to keep doing what I was doing and leave everyone else out of it.

I wanted to be a big-league ballplayer when I grew up. But each year, as I got older, I saw how difficult it was. I saw that even being the best wasn't good enough. Being great in Little League was one thing, but you had to go way beyond that. When I was nine years old, we had a pitcher who was twelve, Neal Tenent. Every game, he would strike everybody out. I never got to know him, and never heard of him again, and I thought, "Wow, he was so good, and he never made it..." Well, it was really hard to accomplish. But I did think that if things went well, I could make it to a low-level minor-league team, so I figured I'd just have fun playing and see what happened.

I got pretty good, though, and I was the starting pitcher in my last two years in Little League. At the all-star game, I pitched and batted fourth. I could hit too. Our town newspaper, the *Stewart Manor Mail*, would cover the games. I'd get mentioned, and saved a lot of the articles. I played Little League through the age of twelve. I liked having teammates, that was fun, although I can recall only one friend on the team that I hung out with away from the game.

When I played Little League, my dad would come to the games, but he didn't sit in the stands with the other parents. He would stand way out in the outfield and watch when I pitched. He didn't want to put any pressure on me. I remember pitching one game and looking out beyond the fence in left field. It seemed way out there, and I could see my dad standing there. I never knew if he was aware that I saw him. Secretly, I was glad he was there.

So I had that interest, baseball, very early, and along with that I developed a love for movies. As a kid I got into movies as soon as I started seeing those ads for the horror and science fiction films in the newspaper. I mean, you'd see this monster or this flying saucer, and all I could think about was how it would look on the screen. Ads attracted me to the theaters a lot. I'd get my parents to take me to the double features and see stuff like *Godzilla*, *The Day the Earth Stood Still*, *Forbidden Planet*, and *Not of This Earth*. As an adult, I starting collecting the original posters from the theatrical release from all of those films I'd go to see in the fifties.

They were scary movies then, and I was just a little kid, so I was really into it, sitting in the dark in some theater in Westbury or someplace. I liked being scared, but only in the confines of a theater or at home, watching TV, or years later, a video. Otherwise it's serious and real, and I've had enough of that.

Those movies did that for me even through the early seventies. As I got older, I saw movies all the time. I loved *The Texas Chain Saw Massacre*; it really scared me. I liked it enough that we used it as a song title, which was Joey's idea.

In 1979, I bought one of the first Sony Beta machines for a thousand dollars. The damn thing was so big and heavy. I went over to Crazy Eddie's to get it. I was living on Tenth Street, and I'd spent every cent I had, so I couldn't afford a cab to get it home. I walked a mile, block by block, resting. By the time I got it near home, I could only walk two parked cars before I had to rest.

I also loved to watch *Chiller Theatre* anytime I could. It was on weekends at eleven at night. John Zacherley was the host, and he was terrific. I later met him at a horror convention, and he and I still write to each other. I was a huge fan of his, and getting to meet him was great. He showed all the horror stuff on his show, the traditionals like *Dracula*, *Franken-stein*, and all the *Mummy* features. Those Dracula films, I followed all of those. But I went in cycles for different movie genres. I liked horror, science fiction, even westerns.

By the time the sixties came around, the exploitation films were in, which had mild nudity with some violence, a great combination. I mean, what kid wouldn't want to watch that?

ABOVE: Teenage Johnny. Courtesy JRA LLC photo archives.

I liked those Russ Meyer films, like *Mudhoney*, *Lorna*, and *Beyond the Valley of the Dolls*. They were really exciting. And the ads in the newspapers for all of those were great. They made me really want to see the movie. The *New York Post* did the best job with that.

So I had all these interests and hobbies as a kid that I kept even when I grew up. I also collected other kinds of cards, like the Davy Crockett series by Topps. I had a coonskin cap, the whole thing. I get flashbacks to certain cards I had when I go through my illustrated reference books on card collecting. I had some car cards and of course the 1956 Elvis cards. I had the Wild West cards too; I think that must have been in the midfifties. I liked those. I always kept my cards nice, unlike the other kids. I didn't put them in my bicycle spokes. I can just see that rookie Koufax card all bent up, just to make a stupid noise. I kept them in boxes, very carefully, and never touched them. I'd just open the packs and put them in order. All my friends collected comics, but I was into baseball biography books and things like that instead.

The Yankees were my favorite team and Mickey Mantle was my idol. My dad turned me on to baseball. He was a Brooklyn Dodgers fan, and a Yankees fan. When we'd watch the games on TV, he'd make me stand up for the national anthem. I didn't think anything of it at the time; I figured they were standing up at the ball-park too.

I've always loved going to ball games. I remember being at Ebbets Field at a Dodgers game in 1957. I remember Von McDaniel pitching a two-hit shutout. I've even talked to some of the players later on in life, and they knew the game I was talking about and everything. McDaniel was a seventeen-year-old kid out of high school and he pitched a two-hit shutout against the Dodgers. I saved my baseball ticket stubs, but not from the fifties, mostly from the sixties on. If you save the ticket stubs, you can refresh your memory quicker. I saved my concert ticket stubs too. I still have them.

Since I was also into westerns and cowboys and Indians, my parents took me to the rodeo at Madison Square Garden, which had Roy Rogers as a special attraction. I had my Roy Rogers outfit on; I must have been five or six. So Roy Rogers actually stopped and saw me in the front row, put me on his horse, and took me for a ride in front of all those people.

Beginning in ninth grade, for two years I went to military school, first at Staunton Military Academy, in Staunton, Virginia, and then the Peekskill Military Academy, near West Point in New York. It was my idea. I really wanted to do it. At first.

"ROY ROGERS STOPPED, PUT ME ON HIS HORSE, AND TOOK ME FOR A RIDE."

I considered a career in the military. You know, be an officer and retire early. I thought that would have been a pretty good life. But military school was really rough. Staunton, especially. It was full of discipline. They would torture you. If you were in formation and they caught you glancing to the side, they would punch you in the stomach. That's why I switched up to Peekskill. The difference was that at Peekskill we had two hours a week of military drilling, and at Staunton it was three hours a day. Every day, from two to five in the afternoon, military drills with weapons, marching, hikes, the whole bit. I might as well have been in the army.

I played baseball in military school, and that didn't go too well. I ended up having two seasons at Peekskill, playing junior varsity my ninth- and tenth-grade years. The competition was a little tougher, but I was still good. I was a pitcher, but the coach batted me ninth, which I didn't like because I was still hitting well. They used me in relief, and I got a lot of innings. So in ninth grade, I thought, "Well, okay, I'll bat ninth." But the next year, I started to have a problem with the coach, and I stopped going to practice. I'd just go to my room and skip it. He'd started to advise me on changing my pitching motion. He was probably right and knew what he was doing, but I was not into taking advice. I was into rebellion, and I thought I knew more than he did. I started to sour on baseball, and at that point I was left alone—no one would coach me. Basically, they were fucking with me, and they stopped even letting me take batting practice. I knew then that I couldn't make it much further, so I just made it one more hobby. I still played stickball all through the years. I played golf one year

at Peekskill, too, but I was so bad at it that all I could do was throw my clubs. I had no patience for that game.

When I was in military school, the teacher lived on the same floor I did, so I went into his room when he wasn't there. I wasn't sure what I was looking for, but I knew when I'd found it—the answer forms to all the tests for the year. At the time, I was skimming along with a 65 average, barely, not doing much at all. I had the ability to be a good student, but I was determined that I would get through everything without doing much. Pretty soon, I was getting a 99 on all of the tests. I'd always get one wrong, intentionally, just so it didn't look suspicious. I was also selling these answer forms to a few students. Not everybody, because then I would get caught. I never got caught this way, and I made a little cash too.

I was glad to get out of there finally, but I think it was good for me. I came back to public school and I was able to coast through doing zero. You can bullshit your way through to certain levels. Past high school it gets a little hard, I'm sure. But in high school, I felt I had learned enough in ninth and tenth grade in military school to get me through eleventh and twelfth grade without doing anything.

ABOVE: Johnny, in uniform (left), and with his father (right). Courtesy JRA LLC photo archives.

Whatever I did back then, I always gravitated toward doing as little as possible. I was very difficult. I refused to answer the teacher's questions and would purposely say "I don't know" to everything. Even if I did know the answer, I would just sit in the back corner, being disagreeable. I would not cooperate. On the first day of classes they'd hand out our books, and I would leave them in my locker and never take them home. I would come to school with just a pen and a piece of paper folded up, and I would try to be defiant. Actually, I guess I just *was* defiant. School wasn't interesting to me. You go to school, and I'm sure it's like this with everybody: You're just too young, and you don't want to learn.

I was starting to grow my hair too. I was sixteen; it was 1964. You couldn't have it that long without getting suspended, not even Beatles length. Just barely over the ears and you could get in trouble. It was rough. It didn't help that my grades were on the low side in public school, either. I spent three years in introductory Spanish. I can't speak a word of it. I liked science and history classes; I did the best in those. But kids, a lot of them, when they're that age, are not ready to sit there and study chemistry or advanced math. Later on, I know I told kids, our fans, to stay in school, and I meant it. But when I was going through it, I just made things difficult for everybody.

I also went out for the baseball team in public school, only this time the coach had a problem with my hair, which I was growing to be Beatles length. He told me I had to get it cut. I couldn't do that, so they cut me from the team. I wasn't going to cut my hair for a coach. Rock and roll had really taken hold of me, and playing baseball took on a smaller part in my life. Stickball in the neighborhood was about it.

My dad also didn't like the long hair, and he gave me a really hard time about it. We had huge arguments. He didn't like the music, either. My mom and dad both complained about the loud music around the house. There were big problems over it.

All my friends—at least, the people who wanted to hang around with me—and I were into the good music like that. Our lives revolved around it. But in Forest Hills in 1964, we were just outcasts. I met Tommy, our drummer, at school. His full name was Tommy Erdelyi. Later on, we bonded over the Stooges and music in general that was aimed at weirdos. At first, he was just another pal. Joey was Jeffrey Hyman, and he was just around. I really met Dee Dee, who was Doug Colvin, later.

My father was from Brooklyn. He had three brothers and they were all tough guys. They'd sit around our kitchen table and drink and talk about things like

construction work and baseball. So, with all that macho stuff, they weren't all that happy when I started to get really into music.

As I got involved, I even played a little bass in a band, the Tangerine Puppets, with Tommy. He was good; I was terrible. I kept trying to play the guitar and couldn't do it. I eventually got frustrated and stopped playing altogether. We had other bands, but they never got out of the basement.

I graduated from Forest Hills High School in 1966 and had no idea what I was going to do. I had a high draft number, 350 or something, and was sure that I didn't want to go to Vietnam. I wouldn't have fled or anything, but I sure didn't want to go to some country I knew nothing about to fight a war. I was in favor of bombing the enemy into oblivion. Same as any war, if you want to be in it, win it. I didn't understand why we didn't just bomb the place out of existence.

At the same time, I didn't really support the war, because I had no idea what we were doing there. It never made any sense to me. But my high number meant that unless the enemy was landing on our shores, I wasn't going to have to serve.

I was just a kid like anyone else. I loved rock and roll music. I started dressing like a rock star even when I was in high school. I was a total weirdo; nobody would talk to me outside my social group.

I worked summers stocking produce at a local market near where we lived, off Yellowstone Boulevard in Forest Hills. I was sort of forming my hoodlum future at that point, and I met some kid at the market who was in one of the Irish-Italian gangs from up on Metropolitan Avenue. I was a leader, not a follower, so joining never occurred to me.

At first, I was going to go to college in Florida, but I came back after two days. I got there for orientation and said, "Forget it. This isn't for me." Then I went to Manhattan Community College for a term, but I didn't like that, either.

The music was always the big deal to me. That, I did manage to be consistent with. I didn't need direction there.

I liked violent bands. I had long hair to my shoulders and all that, like Mark Farner's look when he started Grand Funk. But I wasn't a hippie. I hated hippies and never liked that peace and love shit.

I really didn't know what I wanted to be. So I started acting badly. I got in fights; I took drugs, sniffed glue, Carbona. I got in a fight with a kid one time and hit him, and then his dad came out, and I hit him, too. I took off, the cops came, and nobody would tell them who I was or where I lived. They were scared that I would come and get them if they told on me, and I probably would have. At the age of twenty, I had been on a streak of bad, violent behavior for two years.

I was just bad, every minute of the day. I was a mess at that point. I wasn't working; I was just bad. I was nineteen, and I just wasn't ready for it. I couldn't handle it. I would hang out at the high school at lunchtime, even after I graduated. My mom found some heroin in my dresser drawer, in a little cellophane packet, and flushed it down the toilet. I would see discarded TV sets on the street, and several times, more than once, I took them up to the top floor of an apartment building and dropped them near people walking by on the sidewalk. I wanted to scare them. I spent the night in jail on two separate occasions. The first time, they caught me with some pot, a couple of joints. The second time, they didn't find anything on me, so they planted some pot on me. My folks were embarrassed. They had to come and get me out of jail. My dad said he had never missed a day of work in his life, and he had to miss two because his son was in jail. Two different times, too.

Looking at it now, I think I was tough, but being tough in my neighborhood, which was pretty nice, was not the same as being tough in someplace like the Bronx or some rough part of Queens. So I had the intimidation factor in this very Jewish neighborhood. The other kids just weren't brought up to be tough.

One time, it was the middle of the night, and we wanted to get some drugs out of a local pharmacy. But when we got in, we realized that we had broken into the laundry next door. I was disgusted. We left just as the cops were coming.

But I was the terror of the neighborhood, like a really bad Fonzie. I threw bricks through windows. I beat people up. We also broke into a bakery. I knew the kid that worked there, and he told me he would leave the cash in the register one night, so me and this other kid came back to take it. I watched out while he went into the bakery. But building security came, and the police pulled up, so I ran. They chased me and I got away, but the kid inside ratted me out, so the cops came to my house. I was there alone, since my parents were at work. They took me to the building security guard who saw me and chased me, but he said it wasn't me. He was scared to say it was me because he thought I was in a gang, but I wasn't. The kid who told on me went to jail for a few days. I beat him up when he got out. He died later when he got run over by a car. That's what he gets.

I also did some strong-arm stuff—you know, grab an old lady's purse and run, or punch a kid walking down the street and take his money. I didn't think about it. It was random. I'd be walking down the block, and if I'd see a bottle in the street, I'd pick it up and throw it through someone's window. I was like that all day. I was horrible. I was a horrible person.

I don't even know why I did those things. I think it was just boredom and frustration at not knowing what to do with my life. Tommy wouldn't even hang out with me. Dee Dee I knew then, but not very well. I had another friend, Stuart Salzman, who is dead now. I think he overdosed on drugs. He'd also tried to commit suicide when his girlfriend broke up with him. He called me one day after she left him and asked if I was going to be around later, and I told him yeah. But I wasn't when he called. So he slashed his wrists. He pulled through that one.

I had no idea what my parents knew about what I was up to back then. There I was, out of high school, not working, living in their house. I still don't know what they thought of that.

"I WAS THE TERROR OF THE NEIGHBORHOOD,
LIKE A REALLY BAD FONZIE.
I THREW BRICKS THROUGH WINDOWS.
I BEAT PEOPLE UP."

Then all of a sudden, one day everything changed. I was twenty. I was walking down the block, near my neighborhood, somewhere around Ninety-ninth Street and Sixty-sixth Road in Forest Hills, and I heard a voice. I don't know what it was, God maybe, but it wasn't something I had heard before. It asked, "What are you doing with your life? Is this what you are here for?" It was a spiritual awakening. And I just immediately stopped everything. It was all clear-cut right then. I went home and stopped doing drugs, stopped doing everything bad, and I stopped drinking. I sorted it all out, and a year after that I realized that it was okay to have a beer at night and that I could have two drinks, but that was it. I never got drunk again, because after two drinks, I could feel it. I didn't ever again want to be under the influence. I wanted to be totally under control.

Once I decided to get my life in order, I charted a path to be normal. I wasn't sure I could handle full-time work right away, so I got myself a part-time job delivering dry cleaning. I didn't miss a day's work, and after nine months I was ready for a full-time job. Before that, I had asked my dad for a job as a laborer, and I couldn't handle it. I was not mentally ready, and it was a really hard job he got me, working outside during the middle of winter, laying down pipes and connecting them in thirty-five-degree weather at a place down on Wall Street. The rain came down and froze to ice and froze your hands. I was making a laborer's wage, working mostly with Italians right off the boat. I just wasn't ready. I lasted three months.

Now I knew I could handle it, so I went to my dad, and he set me up with a union job. I had to be ready, because I couldn't let my dad down even more and screw up. After my parents sold the bar in 1961, my dad got into construction. By this time he was a union boss, steamfitters union. So he got me a job as a construction worker. We worked on a fifty-story building at Fifty-first Street and Broadway and another at Forty-second Street and Sixth Avenue. These are buildings that are still there. I was glad for a number of reasons, in addition to the twelve dollars an hour I was making. My dad and I had been estranged after my bad time. This repaired the relationship, when he saw that I could work hard.

Even though Dee Dee lived across the street from me, this was when I really got to know him, working at Fifty-first and Broadway. He worked in the mailroom of the building when I was working construction. This was 1972. We would go to this topless place across the street, Mardi Gras, and have a beer at lunch, talk about music and who we saw play the night before or something.

I did that construction work for five years, never missed a day. So I was really normal. I wasn't sure it was what I wanted to do for a living, but if that's the way it was, I figured, that was my lot in life.

I had other ideas along the way, even as I worked construction. At one point, I thought I would try to own a string of self-serve Laundromats. I figured that couldn't be too much work, other than servicing the sites. I wanted something where I could make a living at it and still enjoy music.

After I graduated from high school, even in my bad period, I went to all the shows. I would check the ads in the *Village Voice* to see who was coming to town. The bigger guitars came along with the Beatles and the Stones. I saw Hendrix shortly after he played the Monterey Pop Festival, at Steve Paul's Scene, among other places. The crowd sat on the floor, and I took a seat right in front of Hendrix. I thought it was tremendous, and he actually made me not ever want to play the guitar. You had to be a virtuoso—then. Even if you had the talent, you'd have to practice for fifteen years before you would get to that point. It was funny seeing him, though. I mean, I couldn't tell if he was great because of all those effects or if he was great because of how he played. It didn't matter. He was just great no matter how you looked at it.

The first concert I ever went to see was the Rolling Stones in 1964. It was their first show in New York, at Carnegie Hall on June 20, 1964. I saw them again, at the Academy of Music, twice. I saw the Who

ABOVE AND OPPOSITE: A few of the countless concert ticket stubs Johnny saved over the years. From the private collection of Johnny Ramone. Used Courtesy JRA LLC. All rights reserved.

a lot, at the Fillmore on their first U.S. tour and when they did *Tommy* live. I saw the Beatles concert at Shea Stadium. I took in a bag of rocks to throw at them, snuck them in under my coat, but they were too far away to hit, like out at second base, and I was in the stands, pretty far back. I had to just watch the show.

I saw Black Sabbath early on, their first American tour. I saw the Doors ten times, and the best ever was at the Singer Bowl with the Who opening. I saw the Amboy Dukes twice. Alice Cooper were tremendous. I bought *Love It to Death*, then went back and bought the first two albums, which didn't even sound like their third album. They really fine-tuned themselves. I saw them live three or four times. The first was at Town Hall on the *Love It to Death* tour, and the place was half full.

I saw the MC5 a number of times. I loved them—they were great. But I always really wanted to catch them on their home turf, at the Grande Ballroom in Detroit. That's where the real deal with them went down.

I bought the first Stooges album at Alexander's as soon as I saw the cover. I just liked the way they looked: tough. I might have read something before that, but nothing had prepared me for the music on that album. I was crazy for it the same way I had been when I'd started hearing those first rock and roll 45s from the jukebox. It was unlike anything I had ever heard; it was just amazing. No matter how cool they looked on the cover, nothing could have prepared me for that. So when the Stooges came to play at the Electric Circus on St. Marks Place, I was there. Ron Asheton came out with his Nazi outfit and made a speech in German. The next day, they went to play some place in New Jersey, and the Jewish Defense League was there to protest.

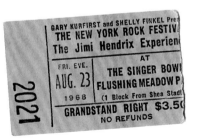

I think that show at the Electric Circus was one of the first times I ever taped a show, on this portable cassette recorder I snuck in. I still have that tape.

I loved those rock and roll shows where you got soaked in sweat and when it was over, nobody could hear a thing, the noise was so intense. Grand Funk at the Stony Brook University gym was one of those. July 24, 1970. That was probably the loudest show I ever saw. I also caught them at Shea Stadium with Humble Pie opening.

Something like Woodstock wasn't for me. I knew people who went to Woodstock, and I knew that I didn't want to sit outside on the ground, in the mud. That just sounded bad. I told them they were crazy. I had seen all the bands that were playing it anyway.

Tommy, Dee Dee, and I would go out to the clubs, which is really how the band got started. We were all friends. We had the same musical tastes, and we liked to get dressed up at one point—in the glitter days. Tommy would always say, "Why don't you and Dee Dee start a band?" And I'd say, "Oh that's ridiculous, that's sick, I want to be normal..." I think Dee Dee always sort of wanted to do it, but he would repeat what I'd say, that he didn't want to be in a band; "We have to be normal," you know, have a job and stuff. Dee Dee wasn't quite as eccentric back then; he was a little saner.

We'd go hang out at this place on Bleecker Street, between Sullivan and Thompson in the Village, called Nobody's. So one night we went, and the New York Dolls were hanging out there. They were already a band, but I hadn't seen them yet. I asked Tommy who this one guy was—I pointed to Johnny Thunders and told Tommy that he looked cool. Tommy said that he was in the New York Dolls and that the band was terrible. But I knew, looking at him, that there was something there, and to me it's always been about the look. So I told Tommy, "No, he's got something going on." He looked so cool, I figured that he had to be decent because image was so important in rock and roll, and he had that.

The New York Dolls really did it for me. I saw them over and over, twenty times in all, starting on August 15, 1972, at the Mercer Arts Center. The last time I saw them was on April 19, 1974, at the Coventry Club in Queens. I keep all this information in little notebooks, which have become known as the "black books." The shows I see, the movies I see, all documented.

I identified with the Dolls crowd. I liked the effect the band had on them, and the look of the audience. They were a good-looking audience, and I thought, "Wow, this looks like fun." It was an event. This was entertainment, not musicianship and people who take themselves too seriously. And for me, it was always about entertainment.

I saw Kiss right in the beginning, and it may sound hypocritical, I guess, but I always thought it was silliness. I have a certain amount of respect for what they've done, but Kiss wasn't cool. The New York Dolls were cool. And that was always very important, coolness. Wayne County was playing loft parties on the Lower East Side with Kiss back then, and I always found him too perverse. There was this ugliness to that. I liked seeing worlds where the girls were all beautiful and the guys all looked like they were in shape and looked a certain way, and to some degree, that's what

I felt like the Dolls attracted. The girls were all dressed up in nice outfits. Johnny Thunders looked good. David Johansen basically looked good. Sure, I'd grown up and seen bands like the Rolling Stones and Jimi Hendrix when their first albums came out. But here, even though I didn't know anybody, I felt like I was a part of it, at the ground level, and that was a totally new experience.

Like the Ramones, who hadn't formed yet, the Dolls, too, were limited musically, but they knew what to do with what they had. When I saw them and realized how limited they were talent-wise, but how fun and entertaining it was, I think that's when it first occurred to me that maybe rock and roll was an option. I'd say to Tommy and Dee Dee, "I can do this too, just as good," and Tommy probably believed me, because he kept encouraging us. Dee Dee and I talked about it for two years sitting outside our job.

ABOVE: Three punk-rock guitar legends collide: Johnny Ramone and Johnny Thunders talk at the Rainbow Theatre aftershow, in London, New Year's Eve, 1977, while the Sex Pistols' Steve Jones looks on (background at far right). Photo by Danny Fields, under license to JRA LLC.

Tommy really wanted us to form a band, and he would be manager, and it would be this primitive thing and so on. We kept saying no, telling him he was sick. I was full of confidence when I would just talk about doing it—you know, "Sure, I can do that." And I could say that as long as I wasn't really doing it. But he kept bugging me, and finally it turned into "Oh, now I have to actually do it?" I wasn't a rock star.

But I liked to dress well, which was part of it, at least the charisma part. I was six feet tall and weighed about 150 pounds, so I could wear a lot of things. I didn't spend a lot of money on clothes, but would always find stuff I thought was cool. Later, when I got a good job, I would get my clothes made at Granny Takes a Trip. That was during the glitter period. I would have them make me velvet suits; I wore snakeskin shoes, chiffon shirts.

I went through phases. In high school, I always looked toward Brian Jones to see what he was wearing and then tried to find the closest thing I could to that. I always thought he was one of the best dressers in rock and roll and one of the coolest guys. Corduroy pants and corduroy shoes and striped shirts and striped T-shirts. Then in 1970 I was influenced by Joe Dallesandro from going to see *Trash*, multiple times, and there was a two-year period where I would wear jean jackets with no shirt, jeans, a tie-dyed headband, and a tie-dyed scarf around my waist. It was the glitter period, in 1972. And I always wanted to be the best-dressed person anywhere I went.

And all through those times, I had a leather jacket that I would try to incorporate into my look. I got it in 1967. I was always my own person. I wouldn't be influenced by what was around me; I would be influenced by something that I thought was ultracool, and take my influences from that. Any show I went to back then—and I was going to them every week—I made mental notes to myself about what I was seeing.

At the same time, I was working the construction job, and I was ready to get married. It was part of getting my life together and being normal. I thought it would be good to be married and set up my normal course in life. Even though I felt too qualified to be a construction worker, I thought, "I don't know what else I *can* do." And I thought that I just had to accept that fate.

When I first started seeing Rosana, she was eighteen and still in high school and I was twenty-two. She was an Egyptian-Jewish mix and reminded me of Sophia Loren. I couldn't believe she liked me. I didn't have anything to offer anybody at the time, and I didn't think much of myself. Now when I look at a picture of myself from then, I think, "Well, I was a pretty good-looking guy." But at that time, I had no confidence in myself at all. We went out for a few months, and then she broke it off. I thought about her for a while and thought that if I got a good car, I'd get her back. This was in 1972. I was working and had money in the bank, so I went with Dee Dee to a car dealership. At first I was going to get a Bentley, but I settled on a Jaguar, which I bought on April 13, 1972. I got there and realized that I didn't know how to drive. So I paid my friend Mark Lester fifty dollars to take my driving test and get a license in my name. At that time, you didn't have a photo on your driver's license. So I went to the dealership with Dee Dee and bought the car for thirty-five hundred dollars, but I didn't know how to drive. I had Dee Dee drive the car home. I really don't know what I was thinking there, but I guess I didn't know any better than to let Dee Dee get behind the wheel. I'd never let Dee Dee drive if I didn't have to. So I drove the car around the block a couple of times, and that's how I learned. Later I got my license in the mail. The night I got the car, I took it into the city to see a show.

So essentially, my life was putting on my jean jacket, getting in my Jag, and going to work with all these union tough guys, then going home, changing into whatever clothes I was into at the time, glitter probably, getting back in the Jag, and driving into the city to see a show.

But the car worked; it did get Rosana back. She saw me in the Jaguar, and she called me within a month—on May 13—and we were back together. I got rid of the car shortly after that. It kept breaking down, and it was eating up all of my money. After all the stress I was having with the Jaguar, I decided to get the cheapest American car. I bought a brand-new red Chevy Vega.

On October 7, 1972, the day before my birthday, we got married. I was twenty-three; she was twenty-one. We got an apartment in Forest Hills at 67–38 108th Street. It was there that the Ramones wrote some of the songs on the first three albums.

Rosana and I would go see the Dolls and any other shows together. We didn't even know anybody else there. We'd get dressed up, drive to the city, see the show, and drive home. And I had to go to work the next day as a construction worker again. I'd go back to putting on my construction outfit, and then I'd get all dressed up and go out and see the Dolls.

But I still didn't want to be in a band.

WHEN AFFIRMATIVE ACTION CAME INTO THE UNION, THEY LAID OFF PEOPLE WITH THE LEAST SENIORITY TO HIRE A CERTAIN PERCENTAGE OF MINORITIES. SO AFTER FIVE YEARS, I LOST MY JOB.

I was an unemployed construction worker from Forest Hills, and I loved rock and roll. And I had this guy bugging me for the past two years to play in a band. I finally gave in.

I bought my guitar at Manny's, on Forty-eighth Street and Broadway, on January 23, 1974. They carry every kind of guitar you can imagine. Mine cost fifty dollars. I picked it out. I liked Mosrites because not many people played them. I got the cheap one. The Ventures and Sonic Smith from the MC5 both used a Mosrite. Those were pretty good references. It was blue. I stuck it in a bag because I didn't have enough for the case. Later I would get photographed carrying it in a shopping bag. I never planned that to be an image.

Tommy kept telling us that he would be our manager and producer, saying, "Don't worry, I'll show you how to do this." So we thought, "Okay, who else should be in the band?" We were friends with Joey and we knew he played drums, and we had another friend named Richie Stern who was into the Stooges like we were. We used to hang out all the time, smoke pot, listen to the Stooges, and Richie would do his Iggy imitation for us.

Dee Dee and I started the band practicing in the living room of my Forest Hills apartment. Both of us were playing guitar, and we were going to teach Richie how to play bass. Joey would play drums, and Dee Dee was going to sing. But after a few days, we realized Richie just wasn't going to get it. He had no sense of timing or rhythm. I was still terrible, but getting better and better each day. I realized I wanted to be the only guitar player in the band, so we got rid of Richie and moved Dee Dee over to bass. We'd be a trio.

On Sunday, January 27, just four days after I bought my guitar, the band rehearsed at Performance Studios, at 23 East Twentieth Street between Broadway and Park Avenue South. The New York Dolls and Blondie also rehearsed there. Tommy and his friend Monte Melnick had built and managed the place for the owners. Tommy got us in for free, and Monte would later start helping out as our roadie. I knew no songs, really, and I didn't know how to play anyone else's. I had to write my own or learn songs that someone showed me that were simple enough. I had no patience at all, but I really wanted to be good. I even practiced at home.

Soon we had two songs that Dee Dee, Joey, and I came up with when we'd practiced in my living room. They were "I Don't Wanna Get Involved with You," which we never recorded, and "I Don't Wanna Walk Around with You," which was on the first album. So we did those two songs over and over. By the way, those songs had more than three chords. We got tagged as being a "three-chord band"

early on by critics who didn't know how else to put us down. But most Ramones songs, even to the end, had more than three chords.

We quickly discovered that Dee Dee couldn't play and sing at the same time, so we had to make another move. Meanwhile, Joey wasn't working out either—he was bad—and it was getting worse every practice. Our limitations were starting to show.

PREVIOUS: (Left) Live in-studio performance at a 1976 video shoot in New York City. (Right) Live with the Ramones in Boston, circa 1977. Photo by Danny Fields, under exclusive license to JRA LLC. All rights reserved.

ABOVE: (Left to right) Johnny, Joey, Tommy, and Dee Dee wait on the subway platform in Forest Hills, Queens, on their way to rehearsal in New York City, July 18, 1975. Note Johnny carrying his guitar in a shopping bag instead of a guitar case. Photo © Bob Gruen / www.bobgruen.com. Under license to JRA, LLC. All rights reserved.

Two months after we started, on Saturday, March 30, we played at Performance Studios and invited all our friends. We even charged a buck to get in. I don't think they ever went to another Ramones show.

We were a three-piece, and it was bad. Dee Dee still couldn't sing and play at the same time, and I wasn't going to sing. As Dee Dee and I were getting better on our instruments, Joey kept getting worse. His limitations were catching up to him. Tommy said we needed more rehearsing, but I realized that Joey just wasn't right. I said, "Tommy, we need to get rid of Joey. He can't play drums." But Tommy said, "No, he can be the singer." Joey had been a singer in this bad band called Sniper. Tommy said that I should stand on one side, Dee Dee on the other, and let Joey stand in the middle. I wanted a good-looking guy to be the singer. But Tommy said, "No, it will be like Alice Cooper. It'll be good." It didn't take much convincing. I believed Tommy.

From the start, we were aware that our visual appeal was different. It worked and drew what was kind of a geek factor. But I think one of the reasons our audience was mostly male was because girls want to see a good-looking singer. I would hear that over the course of our career on occasion—you know, "How did you select him as vocalist?" At that point, though, it was all Tommy, and it turned out to be a good move.

Then we auditioned drummers, but they kept turning us down. We'd like them, but they wouldn't like us. I think we tried out five, six, seven people. Then one day no one showed up for tryouts, and Tommy just sat in. He'd never played drums before, but it was working. So we convinced Tommy to stay in the band, on drums, and things started gelling. Now we got heavy into rehearsing. And it was the real formation of the band. We were the Ramones.

Dee Dee came up with the name; he was the first to use it. He'd heard that sometimes Paul McCartney would check into hotels using the alias "Paul Ramon," so he started calling himself Dee Dee Ramone. We all decided to adopt the same name. It would give us a sense of unity, and we thought it would help us become more established. It would be much easier for people to remember our names, and we'd automatically be promoting the group anytime one of us went out, everywhere we went. So Douglas Colvin became Dee Dee Ramone, Jeffrey Hyman became Joey Ramone, Thomas Erdelyi became Tommy Ramone; and I was no longer John Cummings—I became Johnny Ramone.

We started developing a song every time we practiced. I was getting by on unemployment and had some spare time. After we got Tommy in on drums, we went from practicing once or twice a week to almost every day. We got more committed because we saw that we were good.

The songs were just pure rock and roll. I never liked blues music, and I really didn't like jazz. I liked Chuck Berry as far as that went, but he was rock and roll, not blues. I liked rock and roll music the way the Stones played it. They made it more interesting. They made it in a way I could relate to, which was what our music was intended to be like. The early rock and roll came from more of a country influence anyway, not a black influence. The Everly Brothers, Eddie Cochran, and Buddy Holly were all more country influenced. I listened to some blues records, and it was great stuff, but I was never interested. I never liked long guitar solos and over-indulgence. Our songs just came from a space of pure rock influence. They had to be simple. We were forced to play that way because of our limited musical skills.

Our first shows were at CBGB's on August 16 and 17, 1974. It was just an old, dumpy little bar on the Bowery, as everyone knows. Hilly Kristal and his wife ran the place, and they had nothing going on there besides winos, so they started letting these new bands play there, like Television and Patti Smith's band. Dee Dee had heard about it, and so we decided to give it a try. It was like a practice in front of ten people. We had gotten a lot better by then, and we had more songs.

At that point, we were still dressed in partial glitter because the Dolls were still the big thing in New York. I had these silver lamé pants made of Mylar and these black spandex pants I'd wear too. I was the only one with a real Perfecto leather jacket—what the Ramones would later be identified with—which I had been wearing for seven years already. We were starting to throw in sneakers, Keds. I also had this vest with leopard trim that I had custom made for me. It was like the thing Iggy was wearing on the Stooges' *Raw Power* sleeve.

We were still evolving into the image we're known for, but it was trial and error at first. We didn't know what to do because glitter was still in. So for the first month or two, we were a little torn on how exactly to incorporate what came natural for us, as well as the glitter. We knew we had to get away from the platform boots and so on, and our look was developing, but it wasn't as important as it would get later. No one was coming to see us. And no band is going to look the same at the first show they play as they do a year down the road.

The first couple of times we played at CBGB's, our set list was six or seven songs long. We started playing there every week, charging a dollar at the door. We'd get ten or fifteen people to show up. Our September 15 show at CBGB's got taped by a theater group that was opening for us, and we watched that over and over. After that clip, we made a lot of changes. Tommy and I would assess what we did and how we could do things better. Then we'd tell the other guys what to do. Joey was still doing these kicks and getting down on his knees and singing and doing this fag rock thing, this dumb stuff. It was really terrible, just ridiculous, and we realized it was no good. So we told him to just stand up straight and hold on to the mic stand. Dee Dee was still playing with his fingers, and we told him that it looked better to play with a pick. After that, we were always taping, whenever we could, looking to figure out what we could improve on. We learned a lot from that. As soon as we looked at that first tape, we realized we had to get uniformed. So we got the costume down better and refined it as we played more and practiced more.

I'd give Tommy a lot of the credit for that look. He explained to me that Middle America wasn't going to look good in glitter and said that we needed a more streamlined image. Glitter is fine if you're the perfect size for clothes like that. But if you're even five pounds over-weight, it looks ridiculous, so it wouldn't

RIGHT: The Ramones —(from left to right) Dee Dee, Tommy, Joey, and Johnny at CBGB's on Second and Bowery, New York City. Photo by Danny Fields, under license to JRA, LLC. All rights reserved.

be something everyone could relate to. It would be limited, and by the time Middle America finds out about the fashion, it's dead already. We wanted something that kids could relate to, something timeless. If we had never been around and came out right now with that same look, it would work.

It was a slow process, over a period of six months or so, but we got the uniform defined. We figured out that it would be jeans, T-shirts, leather jackets—Perfectos, like the one I had—and the tennis shoes. We wanted every kid to be able to identify with our image. And there'd be no problem for kids coming to the shows dressed like us, or anything like that.

Now all the mental notes I had been taking over the years came into play. No tuning up onstage. Synchronized walk to the front of the stage and back again. Joey standing up straight, glued to the mic stand—for the whole set. Keeping it really symmetrical. We studied this. We'd get up there later on and start measuring out things and make sure to close the amp line, and close the PA line, just so we wouldn't look lost on stage. I remember seeing the Dolls opening for Mott the Hoople at the Felt Forum and noticing how lost they looked on a big stage. Nothing looked right. And then Mott the Hoople came on, and everything did.

Some bands blow it before they even play. I mean, the most important moment, the most exciting part of any show, is when a band walks out with the red amp lights glowing, the flashlight that shows each performer the way to his spot on the stage. You come out, no talking, no tuning, and it's crucial not to blow it. It sets the tempo of the show; it affects everyone's perception of the band. It was a requirement we adopted, a regimen that started as soon as we'd hit the stage, to make sure you immediately go into the song and not lose that excitement before you even start.

We established those kinds of things in the first six months. It was basically Tommy and me in control. The power struggle hadn't started yet. Tommy would be in charge of talking to everyone outside of the band, but he knew I'd be in charge on the inside. He'd come back to me with what we were doing, and then I would convince the rest of the guys what we were doing.

We did twenty-five shows at CBGB's in 1974. On November 16 we played Performance Studios again, and we'd continue to go back there from time to time through 1975. We ran the door at those Performance Studios shows, collecting the money. It wasn't much at all; nothing really came in. We just wanted to play there, and it was a bring-your-own-drinks thing. The same people showed up each time. At that point, we didn't even put what we made back into the band.

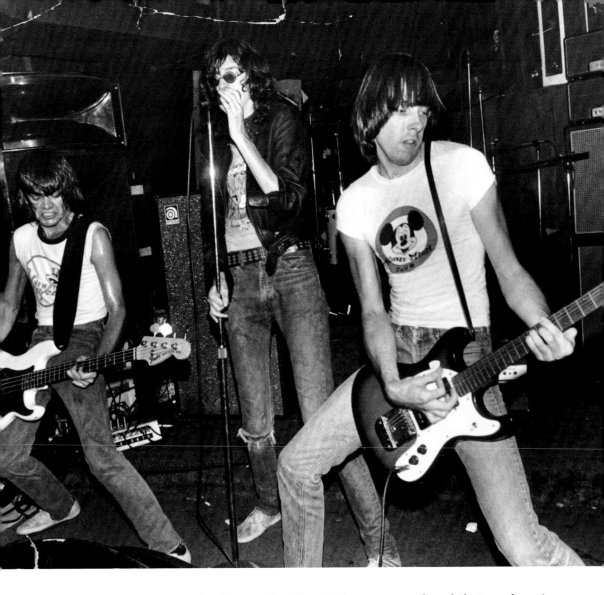

On New Year's Eve day in 1974, I suffered a burst appendix while I was hanging around the apartment. I didn't want to go to the hospital, so all day I lay around with this poison going into my bloodstream. I was writhing on the floor, curled up in a ball.

My wife called my parents, and they came over and told me to get to the hospital. But I insisted on driving myself. I got there and told them I had to get this done and get back home because I had things to watch on TV. I asked if I was going to be out by the next day. I was

"PEOPLE WOULD THINK I WAS UNFRIENDLY, BUT I WASN'T. I JUST DIDN'T LIKE THE PEOPLE I WAS AROUND."

delirious, with a 106-degree temperature. I was in there for a couple of weeks. The only visitors I had were Rosana, Tommy, and my parents.

I never take medication for pain. I want to know if the pain is getting better or worse. I had a crown put on my tooth a couple of years ago and didn't take a needle. I doubt I'll do that again.

I was in intensive care for ten days. My appendix had been burst the whole day, and the doctor said I would have had another hour to live if I hadn't been treated. That's a long time in intensive care. I got out of the hospital on January 15. I was back to rehearsing soon, and I went to see Blondie and Television at CBGB's on the 24th. We played there three nights the first week of March. I was fine.

We were starting to get a little following; people were coming down to check us out. We kept playing at CBGB's and Performance Studios, two- and three-night stands. The people who came were just a bunch of weirdos. Andy Warhol and those people even came down to see us, but to me they were just a bunch of freaks. I wouldn't be very sociable or friendly to them. I just came off as nasty and unfriendly, but they were fine with it. I think they probably wanted the abuse. I met Warhol and he gave me a copy of his newspaper, *Interview*. I threw it in the garbage. Yeah, I watched all of Warhol's movies, but that was make-believe. In real life, it was another story.

But the band was doing well. We were putting up ads all over, flyers, to get people to come to the shows. Tommy was in charge of all that. He'd use the name Loudmouth Productions for the business side of things, so we'd sound professional. Sort of.

We were trying to make it look like there was a company behind us. The name came from our song "Loudmouth," which would be on our first album. Tommy would send out correspondence on Loudmouth Productions letterhead using his real name, Erdelyi, as our manager, to avoid people realizing he was also our drummer.

Lou Reed came down to check us out, and every time we played, a large part of the audience was other bands, always, checking out the competition. I always looked at the Heartbreakers as our major competition. Johnny Thunders led them, so they had to be good. At the same time, they were junkies, so I knew they wouldn't last. They were the next-best band in my opinion, but I knew their career would be short. Blondie was just a lightweight pop band, and no one really cared about them. They became big later on, but at the time, they were just an opening act. The Talking Heads were doing something totally different from us, so it didn't concern me. It wasn't really rock and roll, it was something else.

It was interesting because this was my introduction to a real artistic community, whereas I was from a construction-worker background. I wanted to keep that work ethic, and I realized that this had become a job and I was taking it seriously. I realized that we were very good and that we might succeed.

I mostly went to our shows alone, though sometimes I would bring Rosana. I really didn't talk to anyone. I'd go out to CBGB's and I'd think, "I'm surrounded by a bunch of assholes." People would think I was unfriendly, but I wasn't. I just didn't like the people I was around, and felt that I didn't have anything in common with them. I would go home while the others hung out at CBGB's with the same people, night after night, drinking until it closed. It seemed like a waste of time. I just didn't go by what everybody else was doing. I had no friends involved with the music scene. We were working. CBGB's was where I worked. When I was a construction worker, I didn't really hang out with those guys after work, either.

Ramones songs were basically structured the same as regular songs, but played fast, so they became short. When I saw the Beatles at Shea Stadium in 1965, they played a half-hour show. I figured that if the Beatles played a half hour at Shea Stadium, the Ramones should only do about fifteen minutes. So in the beginning, we kept the set at about fifteen minutes. I'd based it on that. I've always thought you're better off playing shorter. You get in your best material and leave them wanting more. I don't think anyone, even big bands, should play for more than an hour.

Our first label audition was in June with Richard Gottehrer, who was with Sire Records, a little label with big-label connections. He came to see us at Performance

Studios and offered us a single deal for "You're Gonna Kill That Girl." We turned it down. We didn't want a single; we wanted our own album. Then we auditioned for Blue Sky at Performance Studios. And after that, we auditioned for Arista. They passed.

But Blue Sky, which was Rick Derringer's label, wanted more. So they sent us up to Waterbury, Connecticut, on July 11 to open for Johnny Winter at the Palace Theater. Stories, the band who did "Brother Louie," were also on that bill. We weren't even listed. The lights went down, everybody started cheering, and we thought, "Wow, they know about us. This is gonna be great." We were thinking we were big shots, you know. But they thought we were Stories. After a song, I guess we insulted the audience somehow, and then the boos started, and they threw stuff—bottles, cups, whatever—at us. We just wanted to get the set over with as fast as possible and get out of there. It was a disaster. We were not prepared for that at all, but we played great. As soon as we walked off, Blue Sky told us they didn't want us. We got in the van and drove home; it was very quiet in the van that night. We made no money, since it was an audition. I don't recall being really discouraged, though.

It was the summer of 1975 and everything was really starting to click. We'd built a big following and CBGB's was getting packed whenever we'd play. We were the first ones to raise the ticket prices to three, four, and eventually five dollars. We saw it as a business, and we'd have our own person at the door to make sure we weren't being cheated. Less than a week after the disaster at the Palace, we played the CBGB's Rock Festival, with Blondie, the Talking Heads, and some other groups. It became apparent that we were the best there.

Rolling Stone covered the festival with a one-page article. Most of it was about the Ramones, then the Talking Heads, with the other bands just casually mentioned. I thought that we were going to become huge and be the biggest band in the world and change music as part of this massive movement. The Ramones were easily the biggest of the CBGB's groups at that time, so we'd suggest who should be on the bill for the festival. We wanted to make sure it was a good show, and we needed to choose the right bands to help start a movement. I figured that we were going to be playing with these other bands, forming a scene. I had very high aspirations, and I knew that to start a movement, we needed to have other bands and had to influence kids to start new bands. We couldn't be out there like that on our own.

We were also recording some stuff at the time. We did our first demo in February of 1975 at a studio on Long Island, which was most of the songs on the first album. It took a couple of days, and it cost us a thousand dollars. We recorded about fifteen songs at that session; some of those are on the Rhino 2001 CD reissue of the first album.

At the time, we were still looking for a manager that could help us get to the next level, someone with connections. Danny Fields had been a publicist at Elektra Records working with the Doors and was responsible for the Stooges and the MC5 getting signed. I figured, with those credentials, if anyone was going to understand what we were doing, maybe it would be Danny. He was an important person in the scene and knew a lot of cool people, and that was impressive to us. Danny was writing a music column for *The Village Voice* back then, so we would invite him to our shows and send letters from Loudmouth Productions. We met in the spring of 1975 and asked him to manage us. But he was the editor of *16 Magazine* and didn't want to leave his steady job. We were consulting with him for advice from time to time for about six months, but he wasn't our manager yet.

On September 19, we recorded demos of two songs, "Judy Is a Punk" and "I Wanna Be Your Boyfriend," with Marty Thau at an upstate studio. He had been part of the Dolls' management team, but he wanted to be our producer, not our manager. Tommy had the producer role sewed up.

We sent five of the songs we had recorded to record companies, and they quickly sent them back. You could see that the tape was rewound after they had only listened to half a song. They never even bothered after the first thirty seconds. We never even considered that the music was seriously whacked or anything. We were wondering what was wrong with them. We called Warner Bros. and they said that we sounded like bad Zeppelin.

We played three nights, October 3, 4, and 5, at Mothers with Blondie. I had an argument with Debbie Harry over the split of the door money. She thought we were doing a 50-50 split, and I said, "No one is here to see you guys. Everyone is here to see us." We split the door 70-30, and she was mad. I never really got along with her.

We were really good in those shows, and that was when Sire decided to sign us. Our set included songs from what would be the second album as well as the first. We had two full albums of stuff when we were signed. Craig Leon, an A and R man for Sire, and Linda Stein were there, and they presented us to Seymour Stein, the president of Sire, who had us play

an audition. We were offered a record deal with Sire; Danny decided to leave *16 Magazine* and came on board as our manager in November.

In January 1976, we signed our contract at Arturo Vega's loft, which is where a lot of Ramones stuff happened as far as artwork and all that goes. I was pretty happy that day. Arturo was around for a while before I talked to him. He was working for us in some capacity almost from the start. I don't think he was hired. He was just there.

It was a cold winter, and it was freezing out every day we went into the studio to record our first album. I still had the Vega and would drive in to work, which was at Plaza Sound in Radio City Music Hall, where we were recording. I liked working during the day. It was like having normal hours, just like I did at the construction site when I was a steamfitter. My guitar replaced my lunch pail.

We had trouble right away over some of the Nazi stuff in our songs. They were

ABOVE: Johnny with Chris Stein and Debbie Harry of Blondie in the corridor of CBGB's. Stiv Bators (of the Dead Boys) and Jimmy Destri (of Blondie) talk at far right. Photo by Stephanie Chernikowski, under license to JRA LLC. All rights reserved.

really uptight about "Today Your Love, Tomorrow the World" and the line "I'm a Nazi baby." We said, "You're going to interfere?"

We didn't want to change anything. I didn't like the idea that we were giving in, but we made some changes. The line "I'm a Nazi schatze" stayed, so we weren't completely altering the words; but Dee Dee wrote, "I'm a Nazi baby," which we eventually changed to "I'm a shock trooper." We never thought anything of the original line. We never thought it was a big deal. We were being naive, though. If we had been bigger, there would have been a bigger deal made of it by the press. Especially if we were coming out with that stuff now. But Joey, who was Jewish, was singing it. And it was a story about a little German boy in a little German town. We kept to the original lyrics live, though, right to the end of our career. Just compare the opening line of the album version to any live recording of the song in print. I don't know if anyone ever even noticed the difference.

Later on in our career, we had a flap about a line in the song "Wart Hog," which referred to "junkies, fags, Commies, and queers." Gary Kurfirst, our manager at the time, called and said he was getting complaints about the line. By then—this was 1984—I knew better. I said, "Who are you getting complaints from, junkies, fags, Commies, and queers?" I told him there was no way we were taking that off the record. We went without it on the lyric sheet then, which was fine. I didn't care about lyric sheets anyway. Inside the original pressing of the album, it just read, "Wart Hog," with a big underlined question mark underneath the verse. But when the expanded and remastered CD reissue came out in 2002, all of the lyrics were printed. By then the song was a fan favorite. Dee Dee and I wrote it, and it was one of my favorite songs to play live.

The early songs, well, what would we write about—girls? We didn't really have any. We weren't artists or anything, so we wrote about simple things that we could relate to. We thought Communists and Nazis were funny. We thought sniffing glue was funny too, but we didn't even know that people were still doing it. We'd write these songs and laugh, but we never thought we were wacky. We thought we were a normal rock band; but it soon became apparent we were a little off-kilter.

We started recording the first album on February 2, 1976, and we mixed it on the 19th. I didn't understand why it took that long. I was only used to playing live. I thought you'd just go in and play all the songs in one day, and then do all the vocals the next. We were rushing through it because I was conscious that whatever money we wasted was ours and that we had to pay all this money back. So whenever the engineer would ask me how I felt about a take, I'd say, "Oh that's the best I ever played it. I don't think I'll ever play it that well again." And we'd move on.

In the studio, they stuck me in a little room to play by myself with headphones. I thought it was strange, but what did I know? When any questions came up, the other guys would listen to me, and I would ask Tommy. Tommy knew more about what we should do. We recorded the songs in the same order that we played them in our live set at the time, a pattern that we followed when we did the next two albums as well. Even then, the Ramones were a machine of habit.

We had to do a photo shoot for the cover, but no one in the band liked having his picture taken. I'd hated having my picture taken even when I was a little kid, so this stuff was really unpleasant. Roberta Bayley did the shoot. I didn't know her. She was someone who hung around CBGB's and had taken that famous shot of the New York Dolls outside the Gem Spa that was on the back of their first album. She had the credibility, in other words. It was shot in the neighborhood of East Second Street, between Bowery and Second Avenue, not far from CBGB's; the kind of area where you would expect us to hang out. It was bedraggled, with lots of black brick walls, and that worked for us. That's why we took most of those early photos around there. It was perfect for black and white, since there was little color in the neighborhood.

On the cover of the first album, I had my middle finger extended. I didn't have the finger out the whole session, which lasted fifteen, twenty, maybe thirty minutes. But the label used that shot, which was good, though I was really disappointed that no one ever commented on it through all those years. I never thought they would use that one. I was really trying to sneak it in. I felt like I got one over on everybody. But I guess they just expected it from us. It was a good cover, but I still don't think it was as good as *Rocket to Russia*. All I ever said to photographers throughout our career was to get it done fast. We don't need to be paying a bunch of money for a photo.

I never wore a watch. I liked to stay on schedule and on time. I was rarely late for anything. I leave when I'm supposed to leave, and I'm generally five minutes early. Even for the dentist. I was never late for school. I've been like that my whole life.

I always thought that if I were doing something, I should be fully serious about it and do whatever I can to make it good. I felt the same way about my job when I worked construction, even though I never felt I would do it forever. As the first album was being mixed and readied for release, we were still playing any show we could get.

We ordered new equipment after signing with Sire, but it took a little while to come. I opened those boxes with my new Marshall amps at Arturo's loft, where we had them delivered. On May 10 and 11, we played at the Bottom Line with Dr. Feelgood, and it was the first time I used those new amps, four huge cabinets, all wired up. It was deafening. I wasn't aware of how loud they could be. My habit was to crank everything to ten with my other equipment, so that's what I did. I could see the audience leaning back, the noise was so loud. I couldn't hear for a week. I figured there had to be a better way to do this. So I started just going with the bottom cabinets, but kept the other two out there, empty. I always had the amps on ten.

My ears are fine. I don't keep the TV at a loud level. Some frequencies I can't

hear well, and sometimes the phone might ring and I don't catch it right away. If someone is talking and they turn away from me, I might not pick it up.

I saw our first album for the first time at Alexander's, probably the day it was released, April 23, 1976. There it was. It was cool, sort of like the first time I heard myself on the radio. I also knew that we had another one coming out and that it had to be better. It was like one-upping ourselves each time. The albums became a constant quest to make it better.

At first, I thought that the demo we did earlier was better than the album, then I realized that the album was really good. Tommy did a great job.

When I saw some of the reviews, I thought they were funny. Some people would see us as these cartoon rock-music characters, while others tried to intellectualize the record, like it was this big statement. We were really serious, trying to be good. But we weren't thinking of it as anything besides fun rock and roll; we weren't really trying to be anything but that. But as long as people were enjoying it, that was good.

ABOVE: (From left to right) Joey, Tommy, and Johnny goofing around in the studio during the recording sessions for their debut album in February 1976. Photo by Danny Fields, under license to JRA LLC. All rights reserved.

OPPOSITE: Johnny with Joe Strummer, at friend Gerry Harrington's party, April 2002. Used courtesy JRA LLC photo archives. All rights reserved.

The album was out, but we had no tour, and no booking agent in the United States. We decided we should go to England. So Danny managed to get us shows there, and we played at the Roundhouse, then Dingwalls, both shows with the Flamin' Groovies. We did well there. We played in front of two thousand people. It was great to go there; it was a place where so much music history had been created. We went to the record stores, but really all I cared about was playing and coming home. I didn't get real upset about the overseas touring until the next year, when I realized that I really hated not being in America.

When we got to England, we saw that something was really happening there. We hung out with the Damned, the Clash, and the Sex Pistols, and they all came to our two shows. They were all cool-looking kids, which was what we needed for the movement. We were aware that we were changing music by this point, and that we were at the forefront of something new, but we couldn't do it alone. These were people and bands who could help us. We knew that we needed this British invasion. We had based this movement on the Beatles, we were the Beatles, and anybody else was part of it.

That was the first time I met the Clash. Later, when I saw them perform on their tour for the second album, *Give 'Em Enough Rope*, I thought, "Shit, they're as good as us." They were the only thing that ever really came close. I'd seen them during their first album cycle and again later on, when they put too much reggae into their set. But during that tour with the second album, they were great. Every band peaks at some point, and that was it, as good as they would get.

The rest of the year was playing in places we hadn't yet played, like Detroit, Atlanta, and Los Angeles. We moved Monte Melnick from roadie to road manager. We had sporadic booking agents, who would find us shows, then just drop off. We did some shows in L.A. with the Flamin' Groovies, a co-bill thing on August 11 and 12 at the Roxy. We played two nights, the 16th and the 17th, at the Starwood on our own.

We liked L.A. right away, and they liked us. We met Rodney Bingenheimer, who was a really sweet guy. We did his show on KROQ, and L.A. became a very friendly place for us. In all, we did thirteen shows in the L.A. area and San Francisco. During that time, the album made number 114 on the charts. I tracked it all the time. On August 26, we went to Disneyland. I always liked that place, loved riding Space Mountain. I like fast roller coasters. I don't know that I cared about going with the band, but I did have a good time. I like those parks. I've been to Disneyland three times and to Disney World twenty times. At Disney World, I like to ride Thunder Mountain and Splash Mountain.

The rules we had set out for touring were already in place. No food allowed, because then the van would smell like food. There was no cigarette smoking in the van, but pot was allowed. Dee Dee had a pot problem; he smoked a lot. When he was in the Ramones, the others tried to get him to stop smoking so much pot, but I thought he was much better off with it. It kept him tranquil.

We'd take our girlfriends on tour, which was sort of different for a band. It didn't matter; we never had that many hot women hanging around our shows, except maybe in California or Texas. Mostly punks and misfits, and those aren't the kind of girls you want. When we played, I would scan the room, for fun, and if there was a pretty girl, I would see her, usually at the back of the club. Maybe that's why the guys weren't really into finding girls. I know that the standards for the road crew had to be lowered, I'm sure. Besides, I'd rather have my girlfriend with me.

At first we shared rooms, Tommy and I, Dee Dee and Joey. But by 1977, we had our own rooms. And when we took our girlfriends along, we had to have our own rooms. We were working steady now, and even though we were making very little money to begin with, there was more of it coming in. So the first thing we did before we took a raise was budget money for our own rooms. There was never any roughing it at all.

There was one thing we had to deal with right away, which was this condition that Joey had, this obsessive-compulsive thing. He had always behaved erratically, like touching things as we passed them on the street. He was also always sick, even when we were starting out, and down the road he forced us to cancel tours. But this problem he had made him late for everything.

We had to have Monte get over to his apartment an hour early just to get him in the van. There is no way for me to understand this affliction, this condition he had. I saw it as being irresponsible and unorganized. I'd see Joey going up and down the stairs while we waited. I didn't bother to ask anyone about it because I didn't care why he did it. I just wanted to make sure we dealt with it and made it to jobs on time. These were the people I worked with, and we had a job to do.

Once in a while, Joey would say, "We can't go this way," or he would have to go back to the hotel. Monte handled all of that. If we couldn't go back or something, Joey would get in one of his moods. I think people could see it too; fans could see him doing all this touching if they saw him out somewhere.

That wasn't all bad. It wasn't as if we were the models of sanity, so if someone thinks he's nuts, great. We are the Ramones, after all. I just didn't want to know about it. I didn't care about him in that way.

But we were never late to a show. We established that early on, that the show was the most important thing.

And no one could get drunk before a show. As far as vices, I would have two beers after every show, a Bud or a Miller or a Coors, something American. Joey always had a drinking problem; he was always hanging out with everybody. Tommy was fine; he had no vices except cigarettes. Dee Dee . . . whatever.

Later in our career, when we got to the nineties, nobody was drinking. Joey stopped; Mark had stopped. Mark slowly developed problems when he joined the band, and he was drunk for some shows. The most beers I've had at a time, since I stopped getting drunk at age twenty, has been three. I've smoked pot all my life. The pot would rarely have much of an effect. To me, smoking a joint was like having a beer. I'd feel like I had a beer.

Maybe pot should be decriminalized, but we sure don't need kids smoking pot all day long. You could never legalize it, because kids would get it for sure then. They can get cigarettes, and there's no reason to think they couldn't get a pack of pot. I don't think pot is good for you. I don't think alcohol is good for you, either, but it's been legal for a long time.

In October 1976, we went back into the studio to record our second album, *Leave Home*. I wrote most of the stuff I contributed at my apartment in Forest Hills, before I left and moved to a place in the city. I had no amp at home, just an electric guitar. I recorded it onto a cassette and played that back at rehearsal. We had better production, we were playing a little faster, and we had a lot of songs accumulated. We were in really good shape for that album. I like it a lot. I think it's one of our best. I probably preferred it to the first album. It took about as long, if not longer than it did recording the first, but I was used to the process by that point. The whole thing went pretty smoothly.

The title refers to the Ramones leaving New York to go on a tour of the United States and the world. But, coincidentally, I had some personal issues at the time. I got married at twenty-three, in 1972, because I thought that was the right thing to do to lay out my course in life. I got bored in that situation in 1976, because I guess I got married too young. Then I got into the band, and all of a sudden I started realizing that I couldn't really communicate with my wife. I was having trouble communicating. I had found someone else. She went by Roxy, but Cynthia was her real name.

I left my wife in late 1976. I moved out of my Forest Hills apartment at first to Gramercy Park, then to a place on East Tenth Street between Third and Fourth Avenue. By now, the band was going well, and the new album was coming out. We ended 1976 playing seventy-three shows. I was sure that we would be big. I thought we'd do this for five years, and then I'd get into the movie business, and be a director or producer of some sort. I wanted to direct low-budget horror films. It was just a thought at first, but I became more serious about it as time went on. I've always had my eye on the future, not so much planning as being worried. I think I became a delinquent because I didn't know what to do and I was scared. So I thought that after the Ramones, I'd have a big enough name that I could work in the movie industry. I saw films as my future, and music for five years. The band was never supposed to go much past that.

OPPOSITE: Live at the Whisky a Go Go, Los Angeles, December 1978. Photo by Jenny Lens. © JRA LLC.

WHEN WE GOT BACK TO LOS ANGELES IN EARLY 1977, WE WALKED ONTO THE STAGE OF THE WHISKY TO THE SOUND OF SCREAMING GIRLS.

It was ridiculous, but at the same time it gave us confidence. We were playing five nights, with Blondie as the opening act, two shows a night, five dollars to get into the place, which held around three hundred. We were starting to really believe we were that good.

Leave Home came out in February, and we did a four-week tour of the United States with it, starting with those shows in Los Angeles. I liked L.A. even back then and said in one interview that I wanted to move there. At the time, I wasn't serious, but it turned out I was.

A couple of weeks before we went on the road in support of the album, which was our first real U.S. tour, we played a couple of shows with Blue Oyster Cult, at their invitation. On February 4, we played with them at Nassau Coliseum, on Long Island, then packed up our gear and played CBGB's with Suicide. The next week, we opened for Blue Oyster Cult in Poughkeepsie. Those arena shows went a little better for us, although we would have more bad experiences in those big places. I never really enjoyed playing them.

Back then, if you got signed, you went on tour with a major group. There were no clubs to play original material. Clubs were basically for cover bands. To play original material in a club was a whole new thing until the scene started developing. And you didn't have that many groups back then either; it was nothing like it is today. We'd go to towns throughout the country and there'd be no bands there, but as we'd leave each one, new bands would be forming. Kids would see us and think, "Hey, maybe I can do that too." That's how it was everywhere the Ramones went. We'd go to the littlest towns, and play the littlest places, and new bands would form.

On March 8, while we were doing the shows in L.A., we met Phil Spector for the first time. He said right away that he wanted to produce us. He kept after us later, and wanted to produce *Rocket to Russia* and *Road to Ruin*, but we weren't ready for that. I never was, even when he produced us a couple of years later. Tommy was still in the band, and he was our producer.

We also went back to San Francisco to play and hit San Jose, Palo Alto, and Berkeley. The West Coast shows were the first real positive reactions we had in the United States outside of New York. It was a good time in L.A. We stayed at the Sunset Marquis and would sit by the pool during the day or just walk around. I never ventured far from the hotel when we were on tour. I'd sit in my room and watch TV. When we played in Europe, I would take a book, usually a baseball or film book,

a biography of some sort. That's because they didn't have television over there, or at least not shows that were in English.

We'd play anywhere we could get a show, and in 1977 we played 146 shows. We played Pocatello, Idaho, driving in a snowstorm. There were three hundred people there. We played at this outdoor place in Austin, Texas, and it was 110 degrees. I felt like I was walking into another world going to Texas for the first time back in 1977. I thought, "Oh, this is weird!" Then I grew to love it, playing the South and playing Texas. I tried not to notice it, but I know we always got some looks in certain places, and when I noticed it, it made me uncomfortable. But really, I knew that the people there were good Americans who just weren't used to seeing things like us.

We dealt with all sorts of things, and we made almost every show. We played anytime, no matter what, for the most part. On New Year's Eve 1981, at Malibu in Lido Beach on Long Island, we played even though I had food poisoning. I was throwing up all night and the whole ride

"I LIKED DOING INTERVIEWS IF THE WRITER WAS ANY GOOD.

I KNEW THAT WASN'T GOING TO BE THE CASE IF THERE WAS ANY QUESTION ABOUT US BEING BROTHERS."

home, but we didn't miss the show. The only times we missed were once in Virginia Beach in 1981, when Mark got too drunk the night before in Columbus, Ohio, and didn't make it, and two shows in Seattle in 1980, when I had some kind of strep throat. The hotel had some ninety-five-year-old doctor come up to check me out. He gave me a shot, and I broke out in red bumps and splotches all over. Nobody wanted to go near me; they all thought I was contagious, so we canceled and made the shows up two days later.

We were always out there playing, and we always made sure we gave the fans what they deserved. So if we missed a show for any reason, we made it up as soon as we could. They deserved that. Especially those smaller towns, where not much happened anyway. Johnson City, Tennessee; Pocatello, Idaho—we played places like that. I liked those places.

If the attendance at a club didn't look right to me, I would question it and see what their excuse was. We were conscious even then about the money, and we established policies that would stay with us throughout our career, like the guest lists. We really didn't accumulate a lot of people along the way. I mean, some of us had friends in L.A., but in places like Dallas or Nashville, we would have nobody. In New York and L.A., we had a limit of four or five tickets per band member. After a while, that guest list comes out of your money.

As our popularity grew, we got more press attention and did more interviews. I liked doing interviews if the writer was any good. I knew that wasn't going to be the case if there was any question about us being brothers.

We didn't want to get portrayed as this dumb group. So we tried to keep the press away from Joey and Dee Dee and let Tommy do the interviews, since he handled them best. During that spring, in April, we played a show in Boston, and the next day these kids from a local college newspaper told us they were scared to get up front because they had heard things about us. They said, "We were standing at the back," and I asked, "Why didn't you come up front? It really sounds better if you get closer." And they said, "We heard that you vomit on the audience." This was exactly the type of thing we were always up against.

We were aware that it wasn't good to be lumped in with these other bands that had gotten some bad publicity. I never understood why we were put together with them in some people's minds. I thought we were fun, although we were also brutal and visceral. But I just wanted us to be a good band and good to our fans.

When we played England and some other spots in Europe, they were into spitting on the band, which I hated. We couldn't get them if they were in the middle of the crowd. If it happened in America, we could get them; it would be an isolated incident. I would get security to get the person if they were spitting at us. It's an insult to the band. If they do something to anyone in the band, they're doing it to the whole band. In England, it was twenty kids spitting. It would ruin the show for me because I wouldn't move to the front because I didn't want to get spit on. I'd look into the lights and try to dodge it if I could.

The first week of April, we recorded "Sheena Is a Punk Rocker," which would become one of our bigger songs. We used it to replace "Carbona Not Glue" on re-pressings of *Leave Home*, because the Carbona Company had contacted us and made us remove it from the album. They thought the song promoted drug use. I thought it was just funny. People were still doing that kind of thing?

We recorded throughout our career whenever we got a break—it was the circuit: record, tour, record, tour. We did well in the studio. I worked fast, and the band was good at it. Joey always took a long time getting lyrics together and doing the vocals, but the songs were written a certain way, and everyone else's parts were always done quickly.

To keep things moving in the studio, some of the time I would have someone else play a guitar part. It was me playing 95 to 99 percent of the time, but occasionally we would use someone else for different reasons. Sometimes another player would bring something different to a particular part than I would, and all I really wanted was for each record to be good. I never saw a problem with this—it would just be a little extra thing to make the song better. I would tell the player exactly what I wanted to hear and how I wanted it played and where—I was right there telling them what to do. We selected guys we knew and people who would be easy to work with.

Daniel Rey was great to work with all the time. We met him early in our career when he was with this band Shrapnel that opened for us a bunch of times. He produced our last album, *¡Adios Amigos!*, and he played the leads. Walter Lure from the Heartbreakers was good to use too. On *Subterranean Jungle*, which came out in 1983, I had him play rhythm along with me because I knew he would do something different. It came out great. It was so sloppy it was funny. But when we put it together with my guitar, it sounded good, because he was playing these two-note things instead of chords. Nobody could play those bar chords like I played them, so he had to do something different. Ed Stasium, another producer we worked with, also played sometimes. He did some of the notes on some acoustic-based songs on *Road to Ruin*. Tommy played the final guitar chord on "You're Gonna Kill That Girl," off *Leave Home*.

It went the same for lyrics. Later on, we used Daniel to help Dee Dee with songs. Daniel knew the band and how it was supposed to sound. We used him because we would do whatever it took to make a good song. The bottom line was that I wanted to have a good album; I didn't have to be all over it. It was also part of the expediency. I just wanted it done quickly. That was the only way we were going to make any money. We could take two weeks to do an album or two months, and it would still be a Ramones album.

I look back and see that we could have taken more time on some things, but we had a small profit margin and had to get it done; otherwise, we'd have been working for free. That's the one thing I might have changed if we had had a hit on the radio. I would have taken a little more time on the recordings and maybe used some different guitars on some songs.

By the time *Leave Home* started to get out there, we were a professional-looking band on stage; everything had come together. Arturo had designed our eagle logo just before *Leave Home* came out, so we used it on the back cover, and we had a professional backdrop now too. That was to be part of our evolving look onstage—the backdrops, the lighting. Arturo was the first guy to really use all white lights to light a band. I liked it because I liked a bright stage.

In April, we left for a seven-week tour of Europe with the Talking Heads. That was two stress factors: the Talking Heads and Europe. I was clinging to my sanity. I wanted to kill myself. It was miserable, and Europe was a horrible place. I hated

the hotels. I couldn't make phone calls home from my room; I had to go to the lobby and then wait in my room to be connected. I didn't want to go out or go anywhere. There was nothing on TV. The food was terrible, all this boiled shit or curry. They didn't even have ice. I mean, who doesn't have ice? I hated Europe.

Jerry Harrison, the Talking Heads keyboard player, made me nuts. If you asked him a question, he would go on and on, talking for twenty minutes on the same subject. They were all intellectuals. Tina Weymouth was unbearable. I told my roadie to get my guitar, and she told me to get it myself. We were on a tour bus, and I hated the bus. We really didn't talk to them much.

I was never rude to the crew. I think if I was a little stern and said, "What are you doing?" or "Don't fuck up," they might have thought of that as rude. But I never yelled at the crew or called them names. The Talking Heads were college-educated folks, and we were street kids.

Because of all this, things were not going well for me, but the shows were great; I liked that part of it. That was the only part I liked. Though later, I got to like a couple of the Talking Heads. But at the time, with all the factors combined, it was hell.

They'd always want to stop and go sightseeing while driving from place to place. When they insisted we stop at Stonehenge, I wouldn't get out of the car, and I was upset that we were stopping to look at a bunch of rocks. If I didn't want to stop, I wouldn't get out. I didn't let my girlfriend get out, either.

Later we went to France, and I couldn't even believe how bad it was. That's probably the closest I ever came to having thoughts of killing myself. Being in France the first time, I thought, "This is the most miserable thing imaginable." I just developed an instant dislike for it. We made this long drive to Marseilles, and they didn't even have the proper electricity to power us up. So there was no gig. And I never wanted to go back. Maybe I shouldn't have felt that way about France, but that tour did it. I was just so miserable. At one hotel, I didn't have a bathroom in my room, there was some toilet down the hall that was filthy and disgusting. At another, I had a shower—right in the middle where the toilet seat was! It was worse than camping out, and even though I've never camped out in my life, this was probably

worse. I told our booking agent that I would never play in France again, but I gave in later on the condition that I didn't have to spend the night there. I don't think I ever slept another night in that country after that first trip there. And look how they ended up treating us, anyway, politically. What a lousy place. I had no interest. We could have been playing Pittsburgh or Paris; it was the same thing to me.

We were in Europe to work, anyway. We did better over there as a band than we did in the United States. We drew more people, at least. But there were towns that were more exuberant all over. I always liked playing Baltimore, and Toronto was good. Germany wasn't so great at first; it got better as the years went on. It was more modern than the rest of Europe. I liked it better than Scandinavia but not as much as Spain and Italy. The food in those countries was better, the weather was nicer, and the people were good too.

The visits overseas really wore me out. I'm so Americanized that anything else was hard for me to deal with. I'd be so frustrated when I'd try to order food and they couldn't understand what I was saying. I'd order ice and they'd give me one ice cube, and I'd have to drink a glass of warm Coca-Cola. It was so hard. We'd go to a fast food place, and I couldn't special-order, like, cheese and ketchup only and nothing else, so it would always come with everything on it. I couldn't eat any of that other stuff, and I couldn't scrape it all off, either, so it just added to my frustration. And you sure weren't going to get someone who spoke English at a Burger King there. You were lucky to find that in the hotels, where people might be more educated. To see anything familiar was good, though, and I don't even eat McDonald's.

When we got back, I was happy to be home. We played more shows right away, three at CBGB's with the Cramps and then on across the United States. In June, we got our van stolen in Chicago. It was one of the two times we got ripped off during our career. They just took the whole trailer. I came downstairs, and there was no equipment truck. I lost my blue Mosrite, the first guitar I played in the Ramones. The insurance covered everything, but it was a huge hassle. The crew took care of it all; they knew what we had and what we needed. Later, again in Chicago, we got ripped off and I was spared somewhat because my guitar was in my guitar tech's room being worked on.

That summer, we were asked to tape a show for *Don Kirshner's Rock Concert*, and I said yes right away. I had watched the show for years, from the time it started in the early seventies, when they had the New York Dolls and Mott the Hoople on, all those bands. It was taped on August 9 in Los Angeles. They wouldn't let our fans be in the audience, so we played for twenty people who didn't seem to know our music. We did twelve songs. I broke a string, and they wouldn't let me restring the white Mosrite, so I used the Rickenbacker for the rest of the set. It was exciting to do it. Kirshner wasn't there, but he probably wouldn't have wanted to meet us anyway.

We came home two days later, and shortly after that Elvis Presley died. It was August 16. I was in Crazy Eddie's buying some records, and the news came on the radio. I had been listening to Elvis at home before I left and had just finished reading *Elvis! What Happened?*, by Red West, so I was a little depressed already. One more icon gone.

In late August, we recorded the music for *Rocket to Russia* in seven days and then took two days for the vocals. We'd go in and play the songs, pretty much in the order we'd written them. It was our greatest record ever. I still love that album.

We did some shows that fall with Iggy Pop in the East and the Midwest. It was with the best band Iggy had assembled post-Stooges, with the Sayles brothers. But the shows were ruined by rock star bullshit. Iggy kept taking lights from us each night, and finally we got to Chicago and we were down to one red light. We told him we weren't going to play. They gave us another light. This stuff happened once in a while, and we were conscious not to pull it. We played with Cheap Trick one time, and the bass player sound-checked his instrument for an hour, so we never got a sound check. I have no idea what makes people do this stuff. This ain't science.

After a show that year in L.A., I met James Williamson from the Stooges, one of the best guitarists of all time. I think he was the first person I ever met who intimidated me. We met him at the club we'd played that night, and Joey and I went with him back to his apartment to listen to some mixes of *Kill City*. Joey brought a girl, and he was talking to her, and Williamson didn't seem to like that. He kept looking at them. He was very uptight. I was trying to listen to the tapes and enjoy it. I always felt he was charming in a way, but he was just so uptight. I don't know if he was under the influence of anything, or just uncomfortable with a bunch of strangers. I respect him still. He was so intense.

The touring machine was pretty good by now. Everybody had their roles defined. I was working; it wasn't fun and games. That was just my personality. Monte wasn't one to cut loose either. I didn't drink; I didn't do drugs. I was much different at home, where I was more relaxed, like most people who work. But I had to keep these guys in line and had to keep their respect. I had to let them know I was in charge and not let them fuck up. I wanted them to go on and be psyched up and ready to do a good job.

And there were times when I tried to have fun. Once, I tried to get the crew to wear wrestling masks that I'd bought when we played in Tijuana. They refused. I said, "This is entertainment; you guys are boring." I bought six of these Santo masks, these red, white, and blue nylon masks, and said, "You have to wear these." I thought fans would see them and start coming to the shows wearing them. I kept insisting, but they didn't know if I was serious or what. Maybe it was a little out of character for me.

I also had to deal with a lot of things. Joey was always sick. Anything he could get, he had. He would have these foot problems, like his toe would be hurt. I told him to cut it off. I mean, it's only a toe. He told me, "That's fucked up." The one time everything worked and no one was unhappy was when we were onstage. There, we all cared about each other.

Because we were doing so well overseas and selling more records in 1977, we went back to Europe in September, came home and did some more jobs, then ended the year in England, where we recorded the *It's Alive* album on New Year's Eve at the Rainbow Theatre in London. I think our peak, our greatest moment, is that New Year's Eve show of 1977 into 1978. I think that's our greatest moment as a band.

The recording of *It's Alive* was probably the best show that the Ramones ever did. We knew they were recording for a live album, and we were ready. Whenever it was important, we would rise to the occasion. I would concentrate more; I would try harder.

If it was a boring show, my mind would wander; I would be thinking about going home, start looking around at girls in the audience. You couldn't help that when you play 2,263 shows over the course of your career. No ballplayer is going out there every day and being as psyched as when they're playing an important game. But when the big shows came, they got my 100 percent concentration. The bigger the show, the better I'd play. It was what I was waiting for, and I'd never get nervous.

This is also why I didn't sweat much when I played. The idea was to stay relaxed, because if I wasn't relaxed, I was going to worry, and then I would sweat. So I tried to always stay under control. I was never nervous for any show we did. I always knew that the fans would like us and that we couldn't do anything wrong. Maybe a mistake or two, but that doesn't really matter. Only if things started breaking down would I get worried, like if the gear started to mess up. Then it was just a matter of finding the problem and eliminating it right away. I would discuss it with our crew before the next show and tell them, for example, that if my guitar goes out, just unplug me and put me straight into the amp. So I never sweat, which you might notice in pictures.

We got that stuff down pretty early, how to handle power trouble, blown amps.

That tour of England, we were really hitting it. There were twenty-eight hundred people at the New Year's Eve show, which was the most we had headlined for. In the United States, the most was fifteen hundred, which we had drawn at a show in Dallas that summer at the Electric Ballroom.

As we got bigger, people got much nicer to us, but I don't think it was ever reflected in our behavior. We kept it pretty quiet backstage. We stayed okay as far as egos go. It never really went to our heads that much because we'd be back in the real world the next day and playing CBGB's. Nothing had really changed. We could play the biggest show of our career, and the next thing, we'd be back trying to get a job in some tiny U.S. town.

For that last British tour in 1977, we got there a day early and saw the Sex Pistols on December 16. After they played, Johnny Rotten asked me what I thought of them, and I told him I thought they stunk.

And they did, although their record is great. They needed some help. I would have gotten them bigger amps, some Marshalls, and had them spread out a little bit. They were always a little out of tune, so they needed a tuning machine, and they should have had a roadie get Steve Jones another guitar when the other one was being tuned. Sid Vicious couldn't play—they were better off with Glen Matlock in the band. They also needed a professional backdrop instead of the painted sheet they used. Overall, they needed a more professional show, and it would have been simple for them to have been better. It's actually simple for most bands to be better. I can watch any band and if they'd listen to what I say, I know I could help make their presentation better. I think my talent always lay in analyzing stuff like that.

In December of 1977, the Sex Pistols were going to be on *Saturday Night Live*, but they canceled at the last minute because they couldn't get visas or something. When the show called us up and asked if we would substitute for them, we said, "We don't substitute for anybody"—and that was the only chance we ever had to be on *Saturday Night Live*. That was it. Good career move. Elvis Costello went on instead, and it probably made his career.

Even though we had no radio airplay, more and more famous people were coming to see us as people picked up on the Ramones. Bruce Springsteen came to see us in New Jersey. After we played, he came backstage to say hello. It was just him and a friend or two. At one point, he wrote a song for us, "Hungry Heart." His manager found out that he was going to give it away to us and told him that he couldn't. It turned out to be one of his biggest hits. He never wrote another one for us.

Elton John came to see us in England. I opened the dressing room door, and there he was, standing outside by himself. I was surprised to see him. I said, "If you want to go inside, go on in." He looked really normal. We took a picture with him.

Marc Bolan came to see us, and he sat next to me at an after-show party. It was a few months before he died, in 1977. He liked to talk about himself and how good he was on the guitar. Thinking now, I should have asked him about his transition from acoustic material to electric.

Joey enjoyed that stuff more than I did. We played on *The Old Grey Whistle Test* in 1978, and Roger Daltrey was on there with us. Joey and Mark met him and didn't like him. I'm a Who fan, but I didn't really care

ABOVE: Elton John (wearing a *Rocket to Russia* button) visits the Ramones at the Rainbow Theatre, December 31, 1977. Linda Stein is to the left of Dee Dee. Photo by Danny Fields, under license to JRA LLC. All rights reserved.

to meet him. I don't usually look up to people, because I know they all have flaws. Later in life I became friends with Lisa Marie Presley, and she introduced me to Jerry Lee Lewis one time. She had taken me to Graceland for a private tour and he came to meet us. He looked like death. He had this pasty color to him, and I have no idea what he was into, with that glazed look in his eyes. It's a miracle he's still alive. It was a thrill though, and that trip to Graceland was my favorite vacation of all time. I mean, who else gets to look around in Elvis's bedroom? Nobody—that part of the tour is sectioned off. No one gets to see it. It was one of the highlights of my life.

It's funny being friends with Lisa Marie. She and Nicolas Cage met at my birthday party, and when they were married in 2002, I was the best man. Lisa Marie called me one day and said if Nic doesn't ask you to be the best man at our wedding, I want you to walk me down the aisle. I was really excited because that would have been Elvis's job. But at the last minute Nic called and asked me to be best man. I was actually disappointed—I would much rather have walked Lisa Marie down the aisle instead.

We started 1978 on a tour with the Runaways, a band of dykes. At least a couple of them were. Dee Dee was friends with them. It went well, and we traveled through the middle of America in the dead of winter. That tour lasted three months, but Tommy was starting to fall apart and have a breakdown. He was becoming catatonic and having trouble dealing with everything. He couldn't take the road. I never really thought he'd leave. I mean, for Tommy to leave, this was terrible. Tommy was fun to have in the band, and I wish he had stayed in the Ramones forever. He was a good friend.

I was really worried when Tommy left, because he had been a buffer between me and the rest of the band. He was the mediator, so problems were going to start; I knew it right then. Tommy leaving was not good.

We were getting ready to do the *Road to Ruin* album and looking for a new drummer. Mark was it pretty easily. I mean, there was never anybody else we seriously considered. There were names tossed around, like Johnny Blitz of the Dead Boys and Paul Cook from the Sex Pistols. But it got down to why the person wasn't good, like Blitz had blond hair or someone had spiky hair. We tried out one drummer, Mark, and that was it. He was in the Voidoids, and we could afford to pay him more. He was a great drummer, so

there was no problem at all, but we had some choices—and we wanted to make sure we made the right one. Mark was fine, but I knew he was drinking, and I knew that it always gets worse. Mark's first show was June 29, 1978.

Mark would eat anything. We paid him a hundred and fifty dollars to eat a large can of cat food. He got sick. He'd eat bugs, cockroaches—anything—for money. Later on in our career, we found this giant beetle, and when we lifted it up, there were all of these little babies crawling around underneath, attached to it. It was really disgusting, and Mark was going to eat it. Everyone was ready to chip in to pay him, but I said, "No, we can't let him eat that, he'll get sick and he won't be able to play the show."

The band trusted me to get them as much money as I could, and we did fine. They never said a word to me about it or questioned me. I was the money guy. Joey was into his money, and he was happy; he always had walking-around cash.

It was the same thing with the crew. We always kept them working and always

ABOVE: Johnny with Lisa Marie Presley at her wedding.

tried to pay them some wage even when we weren't working. We started with a couple of roadies, and we had Arturo and Monte. Pretty soon we had a guitar technician. Soon after that, we got a monitor man and a drum tech. We always had some professionalism in having our own crew and tried to always keep the guys around. We had the same soundman for most of our career, John Markovich, who was really good. I always liked him.

We went through some guitar techs and roadies, but they would stay for three or four years. I know we didn't pay the best, but we only had so much money. And I tried to make up for it with more work.

I would say, "Money is our friend. It doesn't do anything to you. It is good." I used to say that all the time. It was half in jest, though. Of course, money does help bring happiness, but it's not the whole picture. Having good friends and having someone you love to be with. And being healthy. They're all important. No matter what you have, you can't enjoy anything without being healthy. I learned that later in life. Money does make things easier, though. You can be more generous to people.

We made money over the long run while we were still together. I think that when we really got going, we paid ourselves a $150-a-week salary. When we came back from a tour, we each would get another $1,000. And then we started getting merchandise money, which was more than our regular salary.

I was trying to watch the money. Our profit margin was very small, and we took care of the crew the best we could. I would have liked to have taken care of them better. I was aiming for retirement. I wanted to make sure I had enough. We didn't make a lot of money. We were playing clubs, not arenas. No one ever quit, and they would have if they didn't like it. No one ever asked for more. I was doing what I thought was best. Sometimes you're wrong. If I had paid them an extra fifty dollars a week, they still would have complained. We weren't getting rich, any of us.

Later, we did fine. Anheuser-Busch approached us in 1994 and bought a song for a commercial. I thought it was terrific. I liked seeing the commercial, and people would ask me how I felt about it, and I would tell them it was the easiest money I ever made. I never looked at it as anything bad. Sometimes something like that can be lame, but for beer, which is very American, it's good.

I make more money now, years after we stopped, than I ever did while the Ramones were active. We made a lot of money from merchandising even after we stopped. And the records sold better than ever. Maybe everyone really does love you when you're dead.

FOUR ALBUMS INTO OUR CAREER, WE WONDERED WHY WE WEREN'T THE BIGGEST BAND IN THE WORLD.

So in 1978, when Allan Arkush came along and asked us if we wanted to be in a movie for him, *Rock 'n' Roll High School*, we were open to offers. I found out it was going to be a Roger Corman picture, which made it a sure thing. I loved Corman's movies, like *Attack of the Crab Monsters*, *Caged Heat*, and *Death Race 2000*.

We set out to drive to Hollywood to do the movie, and on the way we opened for Foreigner in St. Paul, Minnesota, on November 18. The next day, we drove nine hundred miles to Denver, and the day after that we drove one thousand miles to L.A. We got there and recorded "I Want You Around" for the movie. It was about the third time we had recorded that song.

We had no promise of much money while we were in L.A., so we had to play some shows there to pay the expenses. The band made a total of five thousand dollars for the very low-budget movie.

We moved into the Tropicana Motor Hotel on Santa Monica Boulevard while we worked on the movie. It was cheaper than the Sunset Marquis, where we usually stayed. We spent a lot of time at the pool. Tom Waits had a room at the Tropicana when we got there. We all talked to him, and he was a nice guy. They tore the place down in 1985. Now it's a Ramada.

We kept working on *Rock 'n' Roll High School* even as we played all these shows. That was when we did our three shows with Black Sabbath, another disaster. There was no way we were going to go over with their fans, who were yelling, "Ozzy, Ozzy!" We would come out and play, and it would fly by, and people would say, "What was that?" And by the time we were done, people were either booing or yelling for Ozzy.

I wish I had checked out Black Sabbath, though, because I really liked them when I was a kid. I went to see them on their first U.S. tour and bought all their records through *Vol. 4*. It would have been like seeing legends. But they were the other band, the enemy, and that trumped legend. They were the competition.

Playing with bands like that was really rough because their fans were tough, they threw things, they were excited about seeing their favorite band, and we were getting in the way. But it was easy opening for Foreigner or Eddie Money or Tom Petty. I mean, who's really into those bands? Who gets excited enough about them to throw something or even to boo?

But on July 2, 1979, we played on a bill with Aerosmith, Ted Nugent, Johnny Winter, AC/DC, and Nazareth to a crowd of forty-six thousand people in Toronto.

It was called the Canadian World Music Festival. I saw the other bands we were playing with and I thought, "This isn't gonna work." I complained to Premier, our booking agency, about it, and they said, "We've been in the business a long time, we know what we're doing. It won't be like the Black Sabbath shows. This is Canada, it will be different this time." It wasn't. It was a disaster again.

About five or six songs into the set, the whole crowd stood up, and I thought it had started to rain. Dee Dee thought the same thing, but they were throwing stuff at us—sandwiches, bottles, everything. Then, all of a sudden, I broke two strings on my guitar in one strum. I thought it was a sign from God to get off the stage, because I'd rarely break a string, maybe once a year. So I just walked to the front of the stage, stopped playing, and gave the audience the finger—with both hands. I stood there like that, flipping them off, with both hands out, and walked off. The rest of the band kept playing for another ten or fifteen seconds until they'd realized I was walking off, and then they did too. I wasn't gonna stand there and be booed and have stuff thrown at us without retaliating in some way. We had to come off looking good somehow, and there was no good way to get out of that.

Aerosmith was on the side of the stage watching us. It was so embarrassing. Steven Tyler came back to our dressing room and said, "Oh, I'm really sorry that happened to you." I said, "Fuck that, who gives a shit. Now we can catch an earlier flight home and get out of this stinking country." But Canada was actually great to the Ramones, particularly Toronto. Doing that show was just a mistake. The agency stopped bothering us about playing with other bands after that one. We'd do festivals in Europe, but nothing metal; basically, shows with us headlining or co-headlining. But in 1978, while we filmed the movie, the word wasn't out yet that we were nobody's warm-up act.

The filming of *Rock 'n' Roll High School* was torture, sitting around all the time. Dee Dee was getting high all the time, my girlfriend was drinking, and I just stayed in my room and watched TV. Things were really getting crazy.

We were in a rehearsal studio during the filming, and Mark said he had left his money on the table, about thirty-five dollars, but it was missing. I knew I didn't take it, and I knew Joey wouldn't take it, so there was no one left but Dee Dee. We had everyone empty out their pockets, and I knew Dee Dee had it. So I said, "Okay, everyone take off your shoes," and there it was in Dee Dee's shoe. We had always trusted each other and that it was okay to leave money lying around. At least that's what I thought.

Dee Dee was out of it the whole time that movie was being made. He originally had three lines of dialogue, but they cut it down to one because he couldn't remember them all. "Oh boy, pizza." He got that one out after about forty takes.

I did mine: "We're not students, we're Ramones." That was my film debut. Later, Vincent Gallo got me a role in a really bad movie, *Stranded*.

I was under a lot of stress. I would have my girlfriend, Cynthia, there visiting, then Rosana, who I was still seeing, would come in when I sent Cynthia home.

We filmed the concert sequence for the movie at the Roxy. It took eighteen hours to get the five songs done. They had three audiences come in over that period, a morning one, an afternoon one, and a night one. They charged the afternoon and night crowds to get in, I think three dollars for afternoon, five dollars for night. And we didn't get any of that. I think I let that one slip by me. Like I said, I was under a lot of stress.

When *Rock 'n' Roll High School* came out that May, I thought, "Well, this could be trouble." Critics liked it, though. I was still afraid to see it, but finally, when it premiered in New York at the 8th Street Playhouse, I snuck into the theater after the place was dark and sat in the back row. People there loved it. The movie was better than I thought it would be.

When Linda got in the van for the first time during that West Coast tour, I told her, "You sit in the back row," and she turned to me and said, "Not for long." I thought, "What is this, this girl answers back to me?" Joey told her not to say anything, but she did anyway. I thought it was kind of funny. Sometimes, I would take both shotgun and the first row. I would handle the radio. It was baseball games during the season, and Rush Limbaugh to piss everybody off.

When we got back to New York, there was some tension over Linda. She was with Joey, and I was with Cynthia, but we would all get together and do things. I liked Linda. She was smart, and she looked great, the kind of girl I liked. I was just happy to be around her.

We would torment Monte in the worst ways. Monte was a very good sport, and he did a fine job. He was never great, but he was good. He put up with us; he took care of Joey, and he put up with us. But he was so fun to play tricks on because he'd get so angry. I mean, if we did something to Joey or Dee Dee, they would threaten to quit the band. You could prank Mark, and he wouldn't care. I think he even liked it. So we had to do it all to Monte. He really was our whipping boy.

One time, we rented a van where you could control the radio from both the front seat and the first row of the van, but Monte didn't know it. Mark and I figured it out, and Mark was sitting in the first row of the van seats, and I would say, "Change the channel, Monte." He'd reach over to change it, and the channels would go crazy all across the dial because Mark was changing the channels.

I would say, "Monte, what are you doing? I want to listen to that station," and he would try to change it, and every time he put his hand near the radio, Mark would switch it really fast all over the dial. So we said, "Monte, it must be a magnetic field; it must be from your ring, or your bracelet or your watch." And he would take it off, and the radio would be fine. Then he'd put them back on, and the radio would do it again. He had no idea what was going on. When he returned the van, he complained that the radio was messed up.

Another time, we got a gay porno mag, and there was a photo spread of some black guy. We signed it, "Hi Monte, thanks for the nice time last night, From Dick Black." At the hotel, we told Monte that there was a guy named Dick Black who was looking for him, and Monte said, "I don't know any Dick Black." So we whipped this picture out and handed it to him. The record company reps were standing there, because we wanted to do this in front of somebody. They walked away really fast. I think they were disgusted. We never cared.

ABOVE LEFT: The Ramones, actress P.J. Soles (Riff Randell), and co-screenwriter Richard Whitley relax between takes on the Vince Lombardi High set during the shooting of *Rock 'n' Roll High School*, December 1978. From the private collection of Richard Whitley, used with permission.

ABOVE RIGHT: Linda, circa 1978. Used courtesy JRA LLC photo archives. All rights reserved.

When there was a record company person to meet us backstage or at the hotel, if they got to me first, they'd ask me who to look for and I'd say, "Oh, Monte Noodnick. Just call him Mr. Noodnick."

So Monte would be greeted with "Are you Mr. Noodnick?"

Then there were the less creative pranks. We would put honey on his brief-case handle, honey on the driver-side door of the van if he was driving. We would secretly hang signs on his back at the airport that said, "I'm gay and I take it up the ass" or "I have the AIDS bug up my ass." So he'd be walking around the airport with this sign on him and wouldn't even know it.

We had a voice box that, whenever you turned it over, would say, "Fuck you, asshole." So when we'd get to a tollbooth to pay our money and Monte would say, "Thank you" to the attendant, we'd put the thing behind Monte's head, and it would say, "Fuck you, asshole." It was hysterical, good Ramones humor. The same thing every time, but we always laughed. We shared a sense of humor on things that would not be funny to other people.

We got pulled over by the cops a few times, and it was usually Monte driving. They took Monte to jail one night after a show in Michigan. We pulled into the hotel parking lot, and the police followed us in. We all got out, and they started in with Monte. It was for something ridiculous like going through a stop sign. We just walked away, laughing, as they put him in the car and took him to the station.

We were pretty safe, though, since we had a radar detector. And when we had my pal Gene the cop travel with us, he could get us out of any trouble. Gene would get out and talk to the police, have us sign a photo, and we'd be on our way. He'd talk police-talk to them and show them his badge. He'd come back and say, "I offered them some donuts." Monte hated it when we had trouble. But he stood up pretty well under pressure.

If I yelled at him, it was nothing. I forgot about it five minutes later, but he may not have. It was the same with anyone working with us. I always forgot about it. I don't think I ever really got mad at him. Monte did a good job. Not a great job, a good job. Who am I kidding?—he was a sloth. We'd have trouble with Joey and sometimes Monte would just take care of him. I felt he neglected us. Joey would get a special meal and we would get crap, and the crew would get crap, and that just wasn't right.

But most of the time he made sure we were taken care of while we traveled, and we were never really uncomfortable. He was great about hotels, too. No Hyatts or whatever; it was Holiday Inns, just like those old rock bands like the Who used to stay at. Unless the promoter was paying.

"AS CRAZY AS THINGS WERE GETTING, IT WAS TIME TO DO SOMETHING. THAT HAPPENED TO BE SOMETHING IRRATIONAL."

We loved eating at Cracker Barrel, and Monte found out that we could eat free if we gave whichever one we were at an autographed picture. So we would pull up, Monte would go in with a signed photo, and we got our food. We also liked County Line BBQ in Austin and Cajun food in Louisiana, and we'd go to Dairy Queen all the time. I would purposely buy a large chocolate shake, drink a little bit, and give the rest to Mark. He would be on a diet, so I'd just drink a little, then give it to Mark and watch him drink the rest of it.

Mark was disgusting, though. He had no manners. He didn't even use utensils. One time we were sitting in Cracker Barrel and somebody at the next table had left half his meal there. So we said, "Look, Mark, that guy didn't finish his meal. There's a good meal sitting there." Mark gets up and goes over to the table and says, "You think it's okay?" and eats the rest of this guy's meal.

As crazy as things were getting, we knew we had to have some kind of breakthrough at this point. It was 1979, we had been out there for five years, and we had no hits. It was time to do something. That happened to be something irrational. Phil Spector.

We tried to bond with Spector. We watched the movie *Magic* at his house one night, and we'd go out to dinner with him. One night, Grandpa Al Lewis from *The Munsters* even came over. He'd be okay with us, but he was very abusive to everyone else around him.

He loved Joey and treated the rest of us like we weren't there. He called us "Joey and the Ramones." It seemed that Joey was trying to get some control, and this was helping him achieve that. Phil was

calling him aside, talking in whispers to him. Even when we were all there, we were kept in a separate room. Joey was going along with it.

Joey and I did not get along well after this ... well, at all, really. It was the Spector album that seemed to change things. The situation with Linda and I becoming close friends didn't help, but there was already a problem.

Spector had been after us for a while, since almost the first time we came to L.A. He would say, "Hey, you want to make a great album?" We were trying to avoid him, but we knew we needed a break. Right from the start, he was abusive to everybody around him, except us. I could see right from the first day that this was not how I was used to working. He was painfully slow, and I could envision this taking forever. I didn't want to be living in a hotel for two months doing a record.

He would make us think we were going to change studios every day, so we never knew where we were going in advance. At the end of each session he'd say, "I'm not sure what studio I want to use, so call me tomorrow and I'll let you know where we're recording." Each day, we'd have to call to find out where to go, but we never moved. We'd be at the same place every day, Gold Star Studios. We'd call and he'd say, "Okay, we'll be at Gold Star." Yeah, that's what we thought, since that's where our equipment was set up, but for some reason he always wanted us to think we might move. I don't know if it was drugs, paranoia, or what. He was crazy.

Spector treated the Paley Brothers terribly. He'd make them stand outside our room in the studio, and I'd say, "Come on in," but Spector wouldn't let them in. Somehow Seymour Stein had pushed them on Phil. He said, "You can have the Ramones, but you have to do a song for the Paley Brothers too." It sure wouldn't have been fun to be in the Paley Brothers. They were about to cry.

And he'd scream at the engineer, Larry Levine. He would go into another room all the time, and stay in there for a while. He never ate and never slept. We suspected he was doing cocaine. We tried to get along with Phil, and he would be polite to us but so horrible to everyone else. Even our crew. One day, our soundman, John Markovich, came by, and Phil started in, "Who the fuck are you? Why are you here?" The same thing over and over, for half an hour. We said, "Phil, this is our soundman. Why are you doing this?" But he wouldn't stop. "Who do you think you are anyway? You're nobody." It was awful how badly he could treat people.

After a couple of days, I reached the breaking point. He had me play the opening chord to "Rock 'n' Roll High School" over and over. This went on for three or four hours. He'd listen back to it, then ask me to play the same chord again. Stomping his feet and screaming, "Shit, piss, fuck! Shit, piss, fuck!" over and over. I couldn't take it anymore. So I just said, "I'm leaving," and Phil said, "You're not going anywhere." I said, "What are you gonna do, Phil, shoot me?" If he had, I wouldn't even have given a shit at that point. I just wanted to get out of there.

So here's this little guy with lifts in his shoes, a wig on his head, four guns—two in his boots and one on each side of his chest—and two bodyguards. After he shot that girl, I thought, "I'm surprised that he didn't shoot someone every year." But if he would have shot any one of us, it probably would have been Dee Dee. Somehow, he irritated him even more. Dee Dee drove him crazy; and Dee Dee didn't like Phil either. He would complain that Dee Dee would show up stoned; meanwhile Phil would be drunk.

Then, on top of dealing with the stress of working with Phil, on Saturday, May 5, only five days after we'd started recording, I got a call at noon that my father had died. I was devastated. Seymour Stein called me with his condolences, and I said,

"At least it's my ticket out of here." My dad's death happened so fast. He was sixty-two, and it was a heart attack.

My parents had moved to Hollywood, Florida, in 1976. I went to New York first, then to Florida, then back to New York, then back to Los Angeles to continue recording the album. It was a time where I was lost, and it was almost surreal. Any time death gets that close, it does something to you. It was so shocking. Whenever I'd think about it afterward, for a long time I'd get very upset. I was very close to my father. I idolized him. My two biggest heroes were my father and John Wayne. Anytime I was on the phone with my mother I made sure to talk to him. I always wanted to please him, and to make sure I wasn't a failure. He was a tough guy, and I wanted to live up to his expectations. I had to get back to business, though, after the funeral. I was just going through the motions for some time.

When I got back to Los Angeles on May 11, I thought it was really nice that Linda came with them to pick me up at the airport. I felt like everyone in the band didn't like me at that point, and I knew they didn't want to come, but Linda did. Monte, Linda, and Joey came to pick me up. It meant a lot to me that she came, and I always remembered that.

The album *End of the Century* turned out to be good, but we didn't have a hit. I think it got played on around 120 radio stations, while the others were played on around 35. It charted in England, number eight or something, but who cares about England? We were American. It did have the worst thing we ever did, "Baby, I Love You." And it was my idea to do a Spector song.

I had suggested we cover "(The Best Part of) Breakin' Up." But Phil decided on "Baby, I Love You," and brought in an orchestra to play on it instead of us. It was more like a Joey solo single now. And that was something Phil had been encouraging for a while, saying things off to the side like, "It's all you, Joey." So Dee Dee and I flew back to New York, and Joey was glad we were leaving. A week later, they tracked "Baby, I Love You"—without the Ramones. None of us played on that song, not even Mark. Phil decided to use a session drummer instead.

Then we got to the jacket issue. When we took the pictures for *End of the Century*, at first every photo was taken with our leather jackets on. Then someone said, "Let's take some pictures with the jackets off." I said, "What for?"

The jackets were part of the Ramones. I went through three in our career. One was stolen in Holland, one in Florida, and the last one I gave to Vincent Gallo. So it was out of character for us to be photographed without the jackets, even then.

They said they were doing it just to change things up. I never thought they'd use those photos. Still, I should never have agreed to take the picture without the leather jacket. That day, I had a red T-shirt on. The pictures came back, and the band outvoted me, so we used the shot with the colored T-shirts for the album cover. It was two against one; Joey and Dee Dee against me. Mark didn't get a vote at that point because he wasn't an original member. They said, "Let's get rid of the leather jackets. The jackets are why we're not getting played on the radio." The photo on the inside sleeve, with the jackets, that was supposed to be the cover. I was mad when I got voted down. I think the picture changed our career.

The whole thing stressed me out. There was a power struggle going on, and at that point, they were voting against me on everything artistic. There were a lot of problems starting with *End of the Century*. Basically it was the first real album without Tommy. Even though he didn't play on the album before, which was *Road to Ruin*, he'd still produced it, and he was involved.

After *End of the Century* came out, it was apparent that we weren't going to get all that we'd thought we would. It is a disappointment to this day. Everything came into focus at this point, and I realized our future. My motivation was pretty pure, I think. I used to think about getting bigger just so we could do more fucked-up songs, get to that point where we wouldn't even have to think about what anybody else told us and we could be as sick as we wanted. It was the opposite effect, really. Get bigger so we can be more twisted. No wonder we never went gold. Chasing some kind of commercial success is more like just sitting there ready to give up.

I would never have put out something like a hit song just to have a hit if it wasn't in our style. I would have had to live with that for the rest of my life, and I don't think I could look myself in the eye after I did something like that.

I didn't really like the albums that much anyway after *Road to Ruin*. Even with that one, they picked the wrong song for the first single, "Don't Come Close," which sounded the least like us. They couldn't pick "I Wanna Be Sedated"?

Same thing with *End of the Century*. "Baby, I Love You" was not a single. I really thought that was the end of our career. I thought that the idea behind singles was to have something the kids could relate to as far as the band went. You think they're gonna come to the show and wait for us to play "Baby, I Love You"? If that had been big, we'd have disappointed a lot of fans who came expecting to hear it. I guess I've always thought of us primarily as a live band too. I thought our live show was great.

And I had a hard time really talking up some of those later albums, especially in the early eighties. When we did press for a new album, I'd hear Joey tell people, "This is our best album yet," but I never thought that. I knew some of them were lame. Joey was never ready to accept that we were not going to have a hit single in America. I have no idea how he could think that something we did like *Pleasant Dreams*, with Graham Gouldman from 10cc, would be our best album yet. I mean, this is a producer who had no idea what we were about, a guy who told me to turn down my guitar when we got into the studio because it was humming.

If I did an interview after the release of a particularly weak album, I would say straight out that I didn't care for the album. I said it, and the label never said a thing to me. They knew there was nothing they could tell me. I would tell the truth.

We made a management change shortly after the *End of the Century* album. We started talking about it in 1979, and finally, after about a year, it was time. It was no reflection on Danny. We had to try something else, I guess. I felt bad; I didn't really want to change managers, because I liked Danny a lot, and I didn't want to blame him for our lack of success. But again, just like with the jackets on the cover for *End of the Century*, I was outvoted. Some names were floated, like Dee Anthony and some other bad choices. I thought I might be able to convince Joey and Dee Dee to change their vote if Danny got a new partner, but he wouldn't.

At some point during our career, I think it was around 1978, Danny had taken on Linda Stein, Seymour Stein's by-then ex-wife, as his business partner. She'd always been good to us and was a Ramones fan, but everybody was complaining heavily about her. There were phone bills, cab bills, and all these expenses we were getting that Danny had never charged us for before. It also didn't help that Joey and Dee Dee's girlfriends were plotting and scheming against Danny, because they felt he only talked business with me. The girls manipulated their spineless boyfriends, and Danny was voted out. No one manipulated me.

Mark had no vote, but it wouldn't have mattered even if he did. If he would've said, "Let's stay with Danny," Joey and Dee Dee would've said his vote didn't count. If he'd said, "Let's get new management," then his vote would have counted. That's the way it was. He probably would have gone along with them anyway, but he had no vote at that point. This is how decisions were made, we'd just vote. It was always this way, and it stayed this way until the end.

When I realized that we had to change managers and that our career was not taking off like we thought it should—and I knew I was going to be outvoted—

I pushed for Gary Kurfirst. He'd been managing the Talking Heads, and back in 1977 when they opened for us at the Orpheum in Boston, he made an impression on me. Arturo tried to give the Talking Heads less lights, and Kurfirst got on the case right away. There was a big argument over it, and I liked that he was sticking up for his band.

I'd also known of Gary because as a kid, he lived across the street from me. I didn't know him, but I knew his younger brother. In the sixties, Gary managed Leslie West and the Vagrants and promoted concerts at the Singer Bowl in Queens, like the Doors/Who show. He had a track record, and I was sort of impressed with him.

It was a good change. Once we got Gary as manager, we started making more money. Not long after he took over, we got paid twenty-eight thousand dollars to play Bond's in New York, the most we had ever made by far. But the money was going up by 1981. We made ten thousand dollars playing Brooklyn; Rockaway Beach, seven thousand dollars; Providence, Rhode Island, seven thousand dollars; Philadelphia, seventy-five hundred dollars; and Stony Brook, New York, ninety-five hundred dollars.

ABOVE: Dee Dee, Johnny, and Joey interviewed at the Hyatt Hotel, Los Angeles, January 27, 1978. Photo by Jenny Lens. © JRA LLC. All rights reserved.

Kurfirst was the Ramones manager for about twenty-five years even though we didn't have a contract for the last twenty-three or so. Gary sent us a contract when we first went with him, and we signed it. When it expired two or three years later, we never signed another one. He would send me contracts, and I would just never sign them. He used to bug me about it, but eventually he just gave up. When our contract with Premier bookings ran out in the eighties, they'd send me renewal contracts too, and I'd say, "What do I need to sign a contract for? As long as you're doing a good job, I'm not leaving."

When *End of the Century* failed to have a hit, I realized that we were not going to be as big as I had hoped. Right through to the end, I never again got too excited for success, because up until then, every album we did, we would think we had a big hit single. When we went with Phil Spector finally, people said, "Well, this is the one." There was a big hype about punk rock taking off, but it didn't happen. In England, they promoted punk rock, and everybody had some hits. That promotion was what it took, and that never happened in the United States. And when there was press about punk, somehow we'd get left out when it was positive and included when it was negative. It was a no-win situation.

We knew there had to be a movement for it to take off, and in the fall of 1977 our third album came out at the same time as the Sex Pistols' first one. We thought, "Okay, great. Maybe punk rock now. Here's the movement." But the media started playing up the fashion element. They'd show all these bands dressing in the punk fashion, and we weren't a part of that, so we'd get left out. But when they'd start saying, "Oh, we can't play punk rock," *then* we'd get lumped in. In 1980 we were dropped by *American Bandstand* because Public Image Ltd went on the week before us. They acted like a bunch of assholes, and Johnny Rotten got up on the podium, so they canceled us the week later. We were always getting screwed.

When I started, I believed that if you were good in this business, you would succeed. But it doesn't work that way. It's the bands who get this promotion, this push, regardless of whether they're any good, who often succeed in a big way. Working hard helps, but that's not all of it.

We wanted to save rock and roll. These great bands were our idols. We weren't against anybody. We were against what rock and roll was becoming, which was no rock and roll. That's what we were against.

I thought we were going to become the biggest band in the world. I thought the Ramones, the Sex Pistols, and the Clash were all going to become the major groups, like the Beatles and the Rolling Stones, and it would be a better world, and this would dominate the airwaves. It would be all punk rock, and it would be great. We turned to Phil Spector as a last resort to get played on the radio, but it still didn't happen.

So then it became a matter of this really being a job and working as hard as possible to take care of our fans and also make some money so that I wouldn't have to go find a job after ten or twenty years of doing this. I could just see it. I would go look for work, and people would say, "Well, you want a job? What have you been doing for the last twenty years? Oh, you were in a punk rock band?"

Well, that wasn't gonna get me a job, you know? People would tell me, "Oh well, you're really smart. Don't worry—you'll get a job as a booking agent or something." I just didn't believe that. If I needed a job, no one was gonna hire me. If I didn't need a job, then that's when people would probably make me offers. That's how the world works.

After *End of the Century*, I really started shooting for a financial target. I knew how much I had to make to retire, and I was hanging in there long enough to make that happen. Even then, though, I knew we were better live than most of the other bands out there. I knew we had to make this work—this was our career—so how we handled it would be important.

Around this time, Linda was becoming my best friend. We were around each other for two years before it started to happen. She was still with Joey, and I was still with Cynthia, but we all toured together from 1979 through 1981. We saw each other on the road and back at home in New York. It ended up that we lived around the corner from each other; her with Joey on Ninth Street, and me with Cynthia on Tenth.

By the end of 1980, Linda and I would meet for lunch in the neighborhood in the city all the time, and by 1981, we were pretty openly hanging out. There were other people who didn't want to see us getting together. For some reason, it freaked them out; like my first girlfriend, Arlene. I'd dated her when I was eighteen or nineteen, and she'd left me. And I was determined that, somehow, I'd get back at her for that. I figured it might take years, but I promised myself that eventually, somewhere down the road, I would torture her. And I did. Years later I would lead her on just a little bit, any time I could, even though I had no interest in her. And she was dying to get back together with me.

Arlene is now the wife of Joey's brother Mickey, but when I was having problems in my marriage with Rosana, she kept hanging around waiting for me to leave my wife. I wasn't interested. When I left my wife, I went out with Cynthia. And when I was having problems there and was going to move on, all of a sudden Arlene was back in the picture again—even though she was seeing Mickey at the time. Well, Mitch. That's his name, but he always asks everyone to call him Mickey.

I still wasn't interested, and she was pissed. She would try to pop in and out of my life, but I never got together with her. Linda would come down to meet me, and all of a sudden Arlene would show up. She'd be getting mad that Linda was becoming friendly with me. One time she even came to a show and said, "Why do you want Linda, when you can have someone with an hourglass figure like me?" And this is while she's seeing Mickey! Linda and her girlfriend were right there listening to all of this and laughing hysterically: "Oh my god, do you hear what she's saying?!" Arlene didn't realize it, though.

Mickey always knew she liked me. She'd come into the city with him to visit Joey, just so she could somehow try to find a way to leave there and meet me. She'd always say to Linda, "Oh, let's call up Johnny and see what he's doing." And they'd come down to meet me. Linda and Arlene knew each other, and she knew that Linda and I were friends. One day the three of us went to lunch, and Arlene caught Linda and me holding hands under the table. She looked under the table and she flipped out, jumped up and yelled in the middle of the restaurant, "What the fuck is going on?" It was pretty dramatic. Like I said, I would lead her on a little bit, but each time I was interested in someone else. I had no interest in her.

I basically had four girlfriends in my life, that's it. I'd dated Arlene, then Rosana; and while I was married to Rosana, I started up with Cynthia. She came to the shows and it just happened. Rosana found out because Cynthia forced the issue and called her. So Rosana threw me out. I would still go back and see her on occasion, but I could never spend the night because I was living with Cynthia. There was a point when I was meeting with Linda (nothing physical yet), and at the same time I was seeing Rosana and living with Cynthia. It was very stressful.

But the end result of everything was that Linda left Joey in the summer of 1982, and a couple of months later, I left Cynthia. The whole thing made situations tense in the band, but I tried to be sensitive, if that's the word. In the fall, Linda and I moved into a studio apartment together on Twenty-second Street. Though I'd always have the van drop me off near my old place on Tenth Street as

if I still lived there. Joey didn't know we were living together, and I was concerned that he'd quit the band if he did. Joey would tell everyone, "If I find out they're living together, I'm going to quit."

I had never really gotten along with Joey, but I didn't want to hurt him, either. Joey and I weren't close friends; we were business associates. Besides, if a girl doesn't want to be with him anymore, what is she supposed to do? Stay with him anyway? If both people are happy, then nothing can interfere. But if things don't work out, then there's a problem in the relationship. I thought it was annoying that Linda stayed with Joey longer than she even wanted to, and we put off being together just because we were worried that it would affect the band. We were really trying not to cause him problems, until it just became totally impossible for us. In the beginning, after she'd left him, Linda even lived by herself for a while. Again, just not to cause problems. We tried our best, but you can't live a lie.

Linda and I never flaunted our relationship, and that was a way to get away from trouble. She stopped traveling with us in 1982, and at shows near home I

ABOVE: (LEFT) Linda and Johnny in the 1980s. (RIGHT) Johnny and Linda married at City Hall—note thumbprint at bottom right. Used courtesy JRA LLC photo archives.

would get off the stage, grab my stuff, and go. I was afraid that the Linda situation would affect the band. I looked at the situation like Keith Richards and Brian Jones and the Anita Pallenberg deal, where she left Brian Jones to go with Keith Richards. I didn't know what to do, because I didn't want to break up the band, and at the same time I wanted to be with Linda.

Until I met Linda, I had made no withdrawals from my bank account, only deposits. I'd lived on my per diem and tour money. I was obsessed with saving money for retirement, and that doesn't go well with generosity. But I wanted to impress Linda, so I started making withdrawals. I remember making the first one from my bank account—it was painful. Tears came down from my eyes! But I never hooked up with anyone else after I went out with Linda. Obviously, it was meant to be. And we've been together ever since, for the past twenty years.

When I was a kid, I did as much as I could by myself, and I probably just got used to doing whatever I wanted. I didn't realize it until much later in life, but I was selfish; up to the point when I decided to get married to Linda. That was the first time I stopped being selfish. I realized that she comes first. We were married at City Hall in New York. It was just Linda and me, and she brought a girlfriend. I paid five dollars for someone to take a picture of us, with Linda holding a plastic bouquet of flowers. Linda noticed a thumbprint on the photo and said, "Let's take another." But I said no. The first one had already cost me five bucks, and it was taking too long anyway. Linda started walking away with the plastic bouquet and a guy came running after her. I'd only rented them, for fifteen dollars. I said, "Linda, you gotta give them back, they're plastic anyway." That's punk. Besides, I may not have been selfish anymore, but I was still frugal.

I think Joey would have been fine if Linda had gone off with anybody else, but it really bothered him that it was with me. Joey was always that way; he would blame others even when it was his fault. I take personal responsibility very seriously. Most things in life are at the very least in part your own fault, the fault of bad judgment. He did the same thing if he messed up a song and forgot the lyrics. He would say, "Well, it wasn't me." I knew this was something that Joey would get very mad about. I wasn't worried about him being mad at me, but I was worried that he would be angry enough to break up the band. I figured out later that it takes everyone to want to stay together as a band, and even though these were tense moments, nobody wanted to mess up the fact that we were the best at what we were doing.

CHAPTER 5

I REALLY NEVER SAW THE KID WHO KICKED MY HEAD IN. HE BLINDSIDED ME WITH A PUNCH FROM THE SIDE, AND I WENT DOWN, OUT COLD.

Witnesses said he kept kicking me in the head. I don't remember anything.

The van dropped me off on the corner by my old apartment on Tenth Street in Manhattan after we played a show in Queens at L'Amour's. It was around three A.M. on August 14, 1983, and I was going to get a taxi to my apartment on West Twenty-second Street. I walked by my old place, the one I had shared with Cynthia, and there she was, drunk, sitting on a stoop across the street. She was with this kid who I had never seen before, a punk rock kid who looked like any other. I thought he would be too intimidated by my showing up to do anything to me. I told Cynthia to go inside, and this kid starts telling me to get lost. I ignored him and tried to tell her that she shouldn't be sitting outside. Even though I'd left Cynthia, I still felt very bad for her. Her drinking problem was really out of control.

The next thing I knew, I woke up in St. Vincent's Hospital, but they had to tell me where I was. My head was bandaged. They were giving me antiseizure medicine, afraid that the injury would trigger some response. My hair was cut off. I had bleeding on the brain, and the doctors thought I was going to die. Again.

I'd suffered a fractured skull, and underwent brain surgery. It even made the cover of the *New York Post*. My mom, Tommy, and Linda came to visit me, and I got a lot of flowers from fans all over the world. I told the nurses to give them to some of the other people in the hospital who were in worse shape than I was. I was in the hospital for ten days. Then I had to take it easy for a little bit. I was ready to play in three months, and our next album would be titled *Too Tough to Die*.

I was thankful that I didn't have brain damage and that I was okay, but other people said that they saw something different about me after the attack. They thought that it had changed me. I didn't feel any different, but I began to be more cautious, and looked to avoid confrontational situations. I didn't back down, of course, because New York is a confrontational place. But I watched situations more carefully, even people around the Ramones who might want to get too close. I did not want to get into another fight. I saw the damage that it had done. I was now more vulnerable to head injuries.

The guy who attacked me was charged with first-degree assault and sentenced to a few months in jail the next year. I went to court and testified. I never heard from him again. I was very angry. I wanted him killed. I'm all for capital punishment.

I think it should be televised. I think they could make it a pay-per-view event and give the money to the victims' families.

So then I fantasized about getting a gun. I thought it would be great to have somebody try to mess with me and kill him. I mean, Bernhard Goetz was a hero. He did what everyone else wants to do. He was Charles Bronson. In real life, who the hell would want to approach Charles Bronson? They go for the Bernhard Goetzes of the world.

After that attack, I was living in New York, and I still loved it, but now I was thinking more about danger. It's odd how something like that changes you. I think I got a little softer. I kept thinking how I could go around the system, like Goetz did. He didn't worry about gun laws. He was the law. In the end, though, I never owned a gun. It was just a fantasy. I was no Charles Bronson.

I think the jury system is a mess. I've never served on a jury in my life. They send summonses to me and I refuse. People have come to my house with a summons and I tell them there's no John Cummings here. I feel offended that they even bother me. I've been ignoring this my whole life. The jury system should be three well-paid people who do this all the time. How do you get twelve people to agree on something? It's ridiculous that a jury is made up of twelve people who are too dumb to be able to get out of jury duty. These are people who hate their jobs and want to get paid twenty dollars a day to sit around trying to agree on something. I'm amazed that anyone is ever found guilty of anything.

But I've always been like that. Somehow, I have to beat the system. It makes me feel good about myself. I can't follow orders. On the other hand, if it's my own initiative, I'm gung ho. Like the Ramones.

A simple example is when I lived in New York, in the late eighties, I found out that Connecticut turnpike tokens worked in the subway, and they were only fifteen cents. You could really save some money. So I went out and bought a bunch of those tokens. Here I was with almost a million dollars in the bank, and I'd be sneaking onto the subway. It was all part of beating the system. The cops were still watching the turnstiles in the subway back then, so I'd walk up with a real token in my hand just in case. At the same time, I always hated turnstile jumpers. What a loser way to do it. You should be able to think your way around the system. It was something that I never outgrew, just getting around the way things were set up. Who are they to tell me how to do things anyway?

When I got out of the hospital after that fight in New York, I started to think more about how to handle the street and be safe, so I wouldn't get jumped again. Later on, I scored some mace, the same police-issue mace that was fired into the crowd and sent everyone running when we played Washington, D.C., that night in the early nineties. I got it to carry around New York in my bag, and one time I really did have to use it in self-defense.

I had just gotten out of a cab near my apartment on Twenty-second Street after a show, and there was this gay bar, Rawhide, on the corner. I called Linda before heading back because I was going to the store and I wanted to see if she needed anything. And some queer came out of the bar and started insulting me, saying, "Fuck you, fuck you, you asshole." And I'm just using the phone. He was drunk and high and all kinds of messed up, and he started coming toward me. I didn't know what he was going to do, so I pulled the mace out of my bag and hit him with it, but it had no effect. He was two feet away, and I kept spraying him, and he kept coming. He wouldn't go down. I got nervous; I was really scared of him. He kept yelling like a crazy person, and I moved away, but he was moving into the street, still coming at me, yelling. I knew I could take him, but I was still nervous and thinking, "What if he comes right at me? Do I have to kill him?" I was glad to get away from him. I walked home. I liked that mace. It made me a little more confident that I had some kind of weapon to keep things even on the street.

For all the bullshit, New York was a great place to live, and I got to spend a little more time there in the eighties and part of the nineties. The band was doing well; I was starting to save a little money. I was investing, and I kept buying bonds. I put a small amount in the market; it was 25 percent into funds or stocks and 75 percent into bonds. So my investments remained stable and kept the risk low. My money was growing, and I had a dollar figure, one million, that I was aiming for, and retirement was becoming a reality. I spent a little money for the first time in the early nineties.

By the mideighties, I was also starting to know more people in New York. I was out all the time. I would walk everywhere, stop and grab a pizza slice somewhere, and keep walking. New York cops would see me walking and ask if I needed a ride. I would put them on the guest list for a show and ask them to come backstage afterward, but they never did. I think they were afraid of what they would see. I would tell them, "Nothing is going on," but they just didn't believe that.

One of the things I am most proud of that we did was a benefit at CBGB's for the New York Police Department so they could get bulletproof vests. It was on April 10, 1979. We even had protesters outside the club, these Commies. I later heard

"WE DID A BENEFIT FOR THE NEW YORK POLICE DEPARTMENT SO THEY COULD GET BULLETPROOF VESTS. WE EVEN HAD PROTESTERS, THESE COMMIES."

that they'd even passed around flyers telling people how bad the Ramones were for having this benefit and helping the police.

The department had some rule that these guys had to buy their own vests. So we got enough money to help out a bunch of these cops. This was when New York wasn't safe at all, before Giuliani fixed it up. The cops became my friends as soon as I stopped being a delinquent. I never worried about them.

The manager at Balducci's, the grocery store in New York, told me I was the nicest celebrity, so he would charge me a bluefish price for shrimp. Sometimes he gave me free shrimp cocktail and charged me two dollars a pound for filet mignon. I think he was a Ramones fan.

The most unlikely place I was ever recognized was on the trading floor of the New York Stock Exchange on Wall Street. I was there with a friend of mine who worked at Fidelity and had invited me to come down and watch the traders. I walked down there on the floor, and everybody knew who I was. They were handing me phones and asking me to say hello to their friends. I talked to everybody. That was in the nineties. I thought, "All these Ramones fans work on Wall Street?" I didn't expect anyone there to know who I was. I think the only place I ever went in New York and didn't get recognized was the Rush Limbaugh television show in 1993. Linda and I went and sat in the audience. No one said a word to us.

I also had some of the perks that doing well offers. I had a beautiful Ford Fairlane, 1958, hardtop retractable, whitewalls, stainless steel, turquoise and white. By then, Linda and I had moved out of the studio apartment into a one-bedroom place on Twenty-second Street. We'd take the '58 Fairlane down to the Time Cafe

at Lafayette Street and Third Avenue during the summer. We'd park right in front and eat at a table outside so we could keep an eye on the car. I didn't need it, but it was a luxury I could afford. I paid fifteen thousand dollars for it, and it cost three hundred a month to park it at our building. I sold it eventually, but not before I restored it for another fifteen thousand dollars. From 1996 on, I got new cars. First a Camaro, then Cadillacs, good American cars.

Most of my friends in New York weren't in the music business. I had friends who shared my interests, baseball fans or movie fans, who had regular jobs. Some were slightly in the movie business as production people. A couple were low-level city employees, blue-collar. I always liked working-class people. When I was in construction, I hung out with the black welders on breaks, and then I would hang out outside with Dee Dee during lunch and after work. I guess I always just preferred the company of regular people when I lived in New York.

While we were still in the band, I never liked to be around people I didn't want to be around, and when I was, it fed my anger. I had to be around the band, and Joey, all the time, so I was angry about that. Likewise, if I went to a club to see a band, I didn't want to see people there that I didn't like. I didn't want to see many people from the past. If it was 1982, I didn't want to be seeing someone from 1977. I wanted to move forward. It was a very general feeling and sometimes even random.

There were people I liked, though, like Johnny Thunders and the Heartbreakers. I never minded seeing them individually or as a band. Dee Dee knew them better because he would do drugs with them, and they were all junkies. When you talk to junkies, it's hard to have a conversation, because somehow their mind will always be on getting drugs. I'd see Thunders in the street or at a club, and we'd talk. The best conversation I ever had with him was shortly before he died in that New Orleans flophouse in 1991. I saw him at the Limelight in New York a few months before that, and we talked baseball. I always liked him and thought he was one of the most influential guitar players in rock and roll. I would have liked to have done a recording with him, maybe a cover song or something, because I always felt that he was sloppy and always had a band that could be a lot tighter. He would have been better playing with me. I could have tightened up one element of the sound.

He was an exception. I really liked talking with him. Others, well, I didn't want to see people from Television, like Tom Verlaine or Richard Lloyd. They irritated me. I hated Mink DeVille. I liked most of the Dictators, but I didn't want to see them out. Richard Hell, on the other hand, I thought was funny; he was a beatnik. The Dead Boys guys, I always liked them. I met Stiv Bators on our first trip to Youngstown, Ohio. I liked him right away. He was funny. One time we were driving along and there he was in the next car, sticking his ass up to the window, mooning us.

I was friends with most of Blondie and the Talking Heads. I think. For the rest of them, I never knew who was in what band anyway. I couldn't keep up. I became friends with Lux and Ivy from the Cramps too. They've always stayed true to what they were doing. We're still friends to this day. Around 1997, Linda and I went to visit them at their house in Los Angeles, and Vincent Gallo came along. He said it was like the Addams Family visiting the Munsters. I took it as a compliment because we were the Addams Family, and I've always loved Gomez Addams.

If Linda and I went to the Limelight, I could walk into the room and everybody would freeze for some reason. People were scared of me. That was the anger I carried around, and it seemed to trouble everyone. It didn't really bother me.

By the mideighties, the band had sort of settled into its place in music. The Ramones were still the best live band out there. And I was starting to see clearly what my financial goals would be and how I could retire. At the end of 1984, I had between $75,000 and $100,000 saved, with a $250-a-week salary plus merchandise money, which was about the same amount. We weren't through yet, and we were selling out most of the places we played, especially overseas.

From 1982 through 1984, we never left the country to play except for Canada, which was a newer market for us. Again, I was content with my life in New York.

We lost Mark for four years while he dealt with his drinking. In October 1981, he missed a show in Virginia Beach, Virginia, and that was his first step toward being out of the band.

We had played in Columbus, Ohio, the night before, and the next day Mark told Monte he would join us in Virginia Beach; he had a ride with someone else. I said, "Monte, what are you letting Mark go with somebody else for? This isn't our policy; this isn't a good idea," but Monte insisted it was okay.

We got to the hotel and no Mark. We kept calling and trying to get ahold of him. It was a nightmare. We went over to the club and waited. Monte finally got him on the phone, but nothing worked; he was still drunk. If we could have gotten him there, he could have played. He was a great drummer. We were ready to get a private plane to get him to Virginia, but we lost contact with him. There were fans outside, and they were rioting. They set fire to something. The next day, we had to play Washington, D.C. We all made it to that show, and then we went home.

I didn't realize yet that we had to make a change, but I was very upset and embarrassed for the Ramones. I fined Mark five thousand dollars for missing a show. We had to drive back to Virginia Beach the next April and play for free.

Mark had a problem. He did his drinking where I wasn't always seeing it. He would tie one on, and then the next day he'd be in a bad mood all day. He wasn't fun when he was like that. It would be awful because if Joey was in a bad mood, it didn't make any difference. I couldn't tell. But with Mark, he was usually fun, funny, and kept things loose. So that would really bother me.

Mark was a different person than Dee Dee or Joey. Mark would work hard. I didn't bully him at all, and part of the difference was that I found him funny. Joey and Dee Dee were intimidated by me, so anything I said was bullying in their minds. But Mark was so goofy that it would be hard to do, because everything was a joke with him. Besides, what could I do about bullying a drunk?

When we were recording *Subterranean Jungle* in 1982, his drinking was really bad. We had to replace him on one song, the cover of "Time Has Come Today." Billy Rogers, a drummer who'd played with Johnny Thunders and Walter Lure, sat in for that one. The producer was telling me that Mark couldn't play. During those sessions, he was leaving early, saying he was tired. That just wasn't like him. Then he'd go out, and someone would see him drinking. So he left us with no choice but to tell him he had to go.

We picked up Richie, a guy who had been around. It was easy and Richie was good. We only tried out two other people. Richie's playing was terrific and he could sing backups. But he left us in a bind in a dispute over money and we lost three shows in New York when he refused to play. He wanted more, and I thought we were still in negotiations. He wanted a piece of the merchandise money. Mark never even wanted that, except for things he was directly involved in, like if he signed drumsticks or skins. I understand that Joey had told someone that we were going to get rid of Richie, which wasn't true. So after about four years in the band, Richie quit, right in the middle of a tour, without any notice; and I never saw him again. He completely disappeared after that. Last I heard, he was a golf caddie.

For a second, right after Richie left, we had Clem Burke from Blondie drum for us. He was going to be Elvis Ramone. He lasted two shows, one in Providence, Rhode Island, and one in Trenton, New Jersey, and it was awful.

He couldn't keep up, not even close. I felt two feet tall when we played those shows. They were so bad I wanted to disappear. Clem was all turned around, speeding up and slowing down. We must have done some fast working, because four days later Mark was back. Joey was all for it, and he knew that it was time. He was smart like that with those changes; it was one of his better qualities.

In 1987, Mark came back, sober, and it was great to have him. What is great is that Mark finally straightened himself out. Remember, he was sober in the Ramones for twice as long as he was drunk.

The biggest blow of all in our career, I think, was the loss of Dee Dee. Actually, he lost his mind in a different way than Tommy. We must do that to people.

First of all, Dee Dee did not play on the last three Ramones albums that he was credited on. He lost interest in playing the bass. He would be in the studio, but he just didn't care. He didn't play and was happy to let Daniel Rey or whoever was around do his parts. Live, we turned him down in the mix, and he could get away with a degree of sloppiness. Yeah, it drove me crazy, but I could cover for him. But worse than that, he wouldn't even move; he would just stand there and not even try.

Dee Dee was getting crazier and crazier, and it wasn't just drugs. By the end of his time in the Ramones, in 1989, he wasn't doing hard drugs anymore. His life was somehow miserable. It was likely the combination of the band and his marriage. He would throw tantrums all the time, yelling, throwing stuff. Most of it he took out on Monte. He was just so unreasonable. He was bloated and just looked really bad—he was on too many medications. This was about the time he got into the rap thing. That was nuts. He shows up at the airport in all his rap clothes, with a big gold chain and a clock hanging around his neck, and he comes up and starts talking like a black person—you know, "Yo, whatsup?"

I was totally disgusted. He was into rap music, which was everything we hated. It sure wasn't Ramones music. It's funny now, but I wasn't laughing then. I told him he had to dress regular, and he said, "Fuck you." It was really embarrassing.

But you know, I never, ever thought of replacing him. He showed up when he

was supposed to be there. He was Dee Dee, our bass player. Most of us at one point said that we were quitting, except me. I never said that. But to hear it from Dee Dee was normal, and I never took him seriously.

I didn't see it coming, but he did leave, finally, in July 1989, after some shows in California. I never wanted him to go. I'd always presumed Dee Dee was staying. We said we were in it together until the end. It was a deal we had. But I think he wanted to try to change his life to the point of having no responsibilities. I've tried to analyze it, and that's the only thing I can figure. And you can't have life without any responsibilities. It's impossible.

Dee Dee had left his wife a month before. We went on tour, came back, and I get a call from Gary Kurfirst's office. I had no idea. *"Dee Dee just called, he's quitting."* I said, "Oh, okay. Fine."—*"What do you mean fine? You gotta come down here, we have to have a meeting."* I said, "I don't wanna come down. He wants to quit, let him quit."—*"No, you gotta come down, Dee Dee's coming, and we have to have a meeting."*—"Okay, fine, I'll come down."

I go down there, and Dee Dee doesn't show up. So I said, "No problem. We start having auditions tomorrow." And that was it. We never spoke about it afterward. What was I supposed to do, ask Dee Dee why he left? Whatever he'd say, it wasn't going to be the true reason. It would be meaningless. If I'd asked him on the day he left, and I'd asked him every year since, I would have gotten a different answer each time. I'd been around Dee Dee for too long to always find these things entertaining. Sometimes it was, but eventually it could just get annoying.

One day, after he left the band, Dee Dee came by the studio, and he was fine. We were talking. When he had quit, we'd made an agreement that he would continue to write songs for the Ramones. His songwriting was still great, and he was very prolific. That day, we were all getting along, but when I left, he flipped out. He told everybody that he hated me and said that he wouldn't write any more songs, and he was mad that we only took three of his songs when he had given me a tape of fifteen of them. But this was all after I left. He would never say things like that to me directly.

Later, we had the *Hey Ho Let's Go! Anthology* boxed set come out on Rhino in 1999, and we had a signing at the Virgin Megastore on Fourteenth Street and Broadway in New York on the release date, July 20. Dee Dee flipped out on the Rhino people while we were doing the in-store, and he was screaming at Monte. I guess they didn't get a car to drive him to the store; he had to get a taxi and couldn't find one. Then he got there and was complaining that my picture was first in the booklet and began arguing with everybody. He was doing this during the whole signing. I was so mad I decided I was gonna hit him when the thing was over. We got done, and I couldn't find him. I would have punched him if I had.

I liked him, though, but he was always a screwup. Sometimes, during shows, he'd get lost on a song, and I'd have to get a roadie to go over there and make him stop playing so I could cover up until the song ended. He wouldn't even know he was lost.

When he quit, people were telling me, "Oh, you can't continue without Dee Dee."

I thought, "I'm not having this defeat me. There's no way I'm having this defeat me. I'll find a young Dee Dee who's going to be cooperative." And I did.

I saw CJ and just said, "He's the one." I knew right away. He looked like Dee Dee, he played like Dee Dee, and those were big shoes to fill. CJ was just out of the Marine Corps, so he was used to following orders. I knew he was going to be perfect. "CJ, just look at the mirror in front of you as we're playing, and you do what I do. You stand the way I'm standing. You move forward when I move forward. You move back when I move back. Just follow what I'm doing." I gave him a bunch of tapes of Dee Dee and told him, "Study these concerts and watch what he does."

By this point, Mark would get a vote, and he was voting against having CJ in the band. I'm the only person there saying, "No, this is our bass player." Mark and Monte were there, and they both kept saying he wasn't the right person. CJ had a mohawk and he played with his fingers, but that didn't matter. They were so shortsighted. We just kept trying out people until I said, "Bring the first guy back." No one liked him again. Monte's sitting there, "No, no, no." Mark's sitting there, "No." I finally said, "The decision's made. It's done. No one's voting." Joey wasn't there. He never even came down to the auditions. We tried out seventy people. It was only Mark and Monte there. Monte didn't count and Mark is . . . This was just a decision I had to make. I said to Joey, "I've found the bass player. Do you want to come down and see him?" The only smart decision Joey's ever made since I've known him was when he said, "Whatever you say is probably right." I guess he knew I had an eye for this. I mean, I could see CJ turning into a young Dee Dee.

CJ added seven years onto the band's life. He was easy to deal with, and he was a nice person. I tried to make him feel like part of the band as much as possible. I hope he felt that way. There are fans who only ever saw Dee Dee as the Ramones bass player. So it was hard for CJ sometimes. I know that for me, no one ever replaced Brian Jones in the Rolling Stones, so I could see that some people didn't care for CJ stepping in. But he was in, and he was it.

I took him down to Fidelity Investments and helped him open an account. Since he didn't make that much money, I felt it was good for him, and it was important to me that when we stopped playing, we all came out of it with something. I couldn't pay that much. The rest of the band would do what I did to save money. They copied me a lot of the time, so I tried to help them all when I could.

"THERE USED TO BE A TIME WHEN EVERYONE IN AMERICA LOVED BEING AN AMERICAN. THEY WOULDN'T WANT TO BE 'ITALIAN-AMERICAN,' OR 'IRISH-AMERICAN.' THEY'D WANT TO BE 'AMERICAN.'"

By 1988 I was really into being home with Linda. We had perfected touring. We knew that we could play one hundred shows a year without really hurting ourselves physically or mentally. I had two hundred thousand dollars in the bank and was looking at that one-million-dollar goal. We had fans, and we didn't need to change things up. Sometimes, I'd tack an extra show or two on without the agency so we didn't have to give them a cut. Extra money, you know.

Our overseas tour money was usually great. When we'd head into customs, I'd rarely get bothered. Joey got interrogated a bunch of times. But I never did, especially coming back to America. They could probably see how glad I was to be home. I'd be standing there in the customs line, and I'd start a conversation with the agents. "Hi, how you doing? It's great to be back in America." Maybe they went through my bags a couple of times, but that's the most they ever did to me.

I remember the two times where I'd felt they'd harassed me the most: once going into Ireland from England, and once coming from overseas into Hawaii. The guy just acted like he hated me because I was an American, and I thought, "Boy, I didn't know Hawaiians hate Americans. I thought you were an American too." But it was still just basically bag stuff, like pulling apart every little thing, and dumping my vitamins out all over the place. I hated that, though, because you know you haven't done anything wrong, and I didn't do drugs or anything; and I'm so pro-America that I would wonder, "How could you pick on me?" But maybe he thought I was a smuggler or something. I think I was coming in from Singapore or somewhere. Landed there for a connecting flight, but hadn't played there.

There used to be a time when everyone in America loved being an American. People would immigrate here and they wouldn't want to be "Italian-American," or "Irish-American." They'd want to be "American." I never considered myself an Irish-American. I don't even see myself as Irish; I look at myself as American.

We had offers to play in Hong Kong, and I always wanted to go there, but I wouldn't agree to do it because it wasn't going to add any more profit to the tour. Even if I wanted to go there, I felt I couldn't play unless we were going to see additional money. It would have added another three or four days on with no additional profit, so I thought, "No, can't go." We never played behind the Iron Curtain either. We had offers, but I refused. I don't know if they could have made me an offer big enough to go. I just expected the place to be so horrible and disgusting, and I felt I'd bad-mouthed Russia so much in the past, I was afraid they might know about that and do something. So I was a little worried about going there, and I just felt like it wasn't worth it. There were enough places for me to go and play.

In Europe I probably looked forward to going to Italy the most, because I liked the food. Then Spain would be my second choice. Scandinavia would be misery to me. The low sky, just clouds and overcast, and if you get too far north, it doesn't get dark at night, or it's dark all day. It was so depressing. The only place I ever really liked when I left America was Japan. It's such an impressive place, and the people are such hard workers. It's so clean. Everything about it is impressive. They'd be so on the ball. I enjoyed it there.

But whether we were in France or in Japan, our fans were always great— although I'm sure nobody in Japan would ever spit at you. That would probably be unheard of; everyone is so polite. I went to a baseball game there, and when they'd hit a foul ball into the stands, the ballgirl would come by, and whoever got it would just give it back to her. They didn't fight over foul balls or anything. The Japanese fans would file into the room before the show. You'd play at seven o'clock at night, with no opening band, and they'd all stand there quietly. Everything would be dead silence, then you'd come on and play a song, and they'd go crazy. The song would stop, and they'd all listen to what you were saying, even if they didn't understand the language. I loved it there. They'd all get the look just right, too. The whole audience would come with the black leather jackets on. They'd all have the punk look down, nice and neat, and perfect—clean. Every little detail. They'd get the buttons on and just really know how to take something and copy it to perfection. Even though they didn't speak English, I'd communicate with them somehow.

CHAPTER 6

THE FANS LINED UP OUTSIDE THE NEAREST 7-11 IN ANY CITY WE PLAYED, KNOWING THE RAMONES VAN WAS GOING TO HEAD OVER THERE RIGHT AFTER THE SHOW.

I'd always stop for milk and cookies to take back to the hotel—my after-show ritual. I wanted to get back and watch *SportsCenter* on ESPN. It was almost the same in any U.S. city, and the fans knew where we were going.

Rock and roll is an unhealthy lifestyle. You have too much freedom. You have no boss, and you can do whatever you want. You can play stoned. You could never go to a real job stoned. And there is a lot of pressure to produce. You can see your career going upward, and then downward, and that can be very depressing. You also get so wound up playing a show that a lot of people need something to bring them down. People who don't know how to handle the situation take drugs. I didn't. I went back to my room with milk and cookies.

I owe my personal success to hard work, intelligence, and luck, as well as knowing how to handle that luck. There's also a certain amount of talent that I'd developed. But most of all, it's the fans. The fans were the biggest reason for the band to stick together and play all those years. I owe everything I have to them. They came to the shows, and any money I made is because of fan support. It was such a good feeling knowing that if I talked to them for one minute, they seemed to be so excited and it would make their day. They were always there; they never deserted us. No matter how hard you work, the least you can do is give back a moment of your time. That meant signing everything whenever I could, and I never got tired of it. It sounds like I'm being silly about this, but I never got tired of fans. I liked them, especially after sitting in the van all day.

I collected autographs myself for a long time, mostly baseball players'. I was a fan, and I knew that I never wanted to be treated badly by someone I might look up to. I would stand in line to get the autographs: Mickey Mantle, Stan Musial, Willie Mays, Warren Spahn. Spahn was always a nice guy; we talked baseball. And he had no idea who I was, which was even better.

I asked ballplayers for autographs even when I was in my thirties and forties. I recall asking Brett Butler for an autograph when he was with the Dodgers and how nice he was about it. I know he didn't know who I was. I also asked Tom Seaver for one as his career was winding down. I was standing there at the railing by my front-row seat, and there was nobody around, but he said, "Not now." If not now, when? I know I didn't want to be like that. I hope I never was.

I always told the fans who had bands to make sure they stayed in school and had a job, and not to make the band their whole life.

I even hired some fans. CJ, our bass player, was a fan before he was a Ramone.

I knew that Rick Weinman, who became my guitar tech, was a fan before we hired him. He would come to all of our Louisiana shows in the seventies. First he sold merchandise, then Arturo fired him, so I gave him a job working for me.

I always took the Baseball America yearbooks on tour. They listed all the games, minor and major league, so I would get the itinerary and see where we could catch a game. Usually, I would key in on a day off and try to get there early. I took people from the crew. I'd say, "There's a game in this city—who wants to go?"

Sometimes people would recognize me at the parks, but I knew all of that came with the territory. I was okay with it. I went to a Boston Red Sox game in 1990, and one person asked me for an autograph. Next thing I knew, there was a line by my seat. I signed for a while, and then I had to leave. We had a show that night, and I only had a half hour to be at the game. That never happened at Yankee Stadium, where it seemed like everybody knew who

I was, but they just said hi. What would have been worse was if I'd gone someplace like Fenway and nobody wanted an autograph.

I always had in mind to treat people like I'd like to be treated. I tell anyone who's becoming a celebrity how important that is. I hope someone pays attention to that.

It had two sides to it, being a little bit known. Sure, there could be perks, but I knew they were treating Johnny Ramone special, not me, really. It was funny. I treated this celebrity status like a joke. I was an entertainer.

Another thing about celebrity was that people would come up to me and say that Johnny Ramone had been at their party the other night. I'd let them know, "Well, I'm Johnny Ramone, and you don't know what you're talking about." But that was that. I never dwelled on it, although I did see it more in Los Angeles than in New York. People would kind of try to use you to get some status in the eyes of others, to show off.

In the early nineties, we were in a club in North Carolina after playing a show, and this kid kept motioning me over to where he was sitting. I ignored him, and he came up to me and asked me to come over and say hi to his girlfriend. I said, "No, you can bring her over here." Then he said he'd pay me to go over and say hi. I said, "There's no amount of money you could ever pay that will get me to do that." So people would abuse the idea of someone being accessible and friendly.

And there were the fans who just wanted to be part of anything having to do with the Ramones. At a packed show in 1988 in Orlando, Florida, a kid spit on Joey, and I was enraged. You mess with one of us, you mess with all of us. It was an insult to the Ramones. So in between songs I said, "Which one of you fucking faggots is doing the spitting? Come on up here!" I'd be very protective of anyone doing anything to the band.

Some guy in the front started raising his hands saying, "Me, Johnny, pick me, I did it," and by the time this kid got the words out, I hit him right in the head with my guitar. Then security grabbed him and started beating the crap out of him. And I thought, "Oh shit," this wasn't even the kid who had spit. He just wanted to be involved. He was volunteering! He probably has a good story about that even today.

As we got older and played with younger bands, I noticed that a lot of them wanted to meet us, almost as fans rather than as the opening, or in some cases headlining, band. While the eighties were pretty down and kind of lonely, in the nineties I started to see all of these new punk groups.

CJ always talked to the other bands, but I would never do that. He was our ambassador. They were still the competition, and I didn't like them. I was introduced to Soundgarden by CJ when I was walking through the hotel lobby in Australia. I was going to walk right by, and CJ stopped me and said, "Soundgarden says they like you guys." So I stopped and talked and found out that they had recorded one of our songs, "I Can't Give You Anything," for an upcoming single. They played the song for me, and they did a good job, so we got along. If they had fucked it up, I doubt I would have spent much more time with them. We hung out for the rest of the tour and became friends.

For most people, there was a chain of command to talk to other bands, and I didn't want to deal with that, so I didn't talk to them. We played with U2 at a stadium after they requested us. Our dressing room was down the hall from theirs, and I know that some of our crew wanted to meet them. But U2 had these big security goons out there blocking off the entire hallway. I didn't like that, and I thought, "This band is not treating people right." I didn't understand why they asked us to play on the bill and then just roped themselves off like that. I didn't really care to meet them anyway.

We didn't have the big security force, but if other bands wanted to talk to us, they would talk to CJ first, since he was out there talking anyway. Everyone got to know how it worked. I had no interest in most of these other bands we were playing with as our time drew to a close.

I noticed that in the nineties more and more bands were telling us of our influence, people like Kirk Hammett from Metallica. Then I met Eddie Vedder and Rob Zombie and realized that these were really our fans, not our competition. I was getting closer to my dollar figure for retirement, and I think I started to feel more relaxed with the whole situation. These bands

ABOVE: Johnny and friend Eddie Vedder visit the L.A. Dodgers dugout. Used courtesy JRA LLC photo archives.

"ECCENTRICS WERE ALWAYS MORE FUN THAN NORMAL PEOPLE.

NO ONE ELSE WANTS TO BE FRIENDS WITH THESE WEIRDOS."

were our fans, and I was becoming okay with it. Pretty soon, I started making friends with some of them.

We toured with White Zombie in 1995. We got to the first gig, and there was a flap about T-shirt booths and where they were going to go and how much we could charge. Some bands wouldn't allow us to sell our merchandise cheaper than theirs, knowing that we always sold much more than almost anyone. So I went to the promoter and said, "Who do I talk to in White Zombie about this?" He pointed to Rob Zombie and said, "Him." So I thought, "Great, now I have to deal with this freak, with his dreadlocks and his beard and his getup."

I wasn't into those new bands a whole lot, and sometimes I would see things I didn't like. We played with the Red Hot Chili Peppers in Finland in 1988. They ran onto the stage with no clothes on while we were playing. "What a bunch of assholes," I thought, and I told them so. They came back to the dressing room to apologize, and I did not accept that. And I was the only one in the band who was really pissed. I got to know them later, and the Red Hot Chili Peppers were cool. Still, what they did that day wasn't cool. John Frusciante and I have become good friends, but he wasn't in the Chili Peppers when that happened. I think he joined the following year.

The people I've always hung out with have been eccentrics in some way, or people that I share common interests with. Eccentrics were always more fun than normal people, though. Usually, no one else wants to be friends with these weirdos. I like that about certain people too. People say that John Frusciante is strange, but I really like him. In *Rolling Stone*'s top 100 guitar players of all time I'm ranked at #16, and Frusciante is #18.

I was slowly making new friends in the same field I was in, and I had never done that before. I knew that there was all this upsurge of respect for us and what we had done. And there were the numerous imitators, these pop-punk bands. I never bothered with most of them. I knew they could never do what I did.

By the early nineties, we'd become really big in South America. I don't know how, I don't know why, but I was really surprised. It was great. We drew much bigger crowds there than we did anywhere. The first time I realized what was going on, I called Linda and said, "Wow, this is incredible. We're like the Beatles here! This is how the rest of the world should be." But soon I was a prisoner. I called her back a few hours later saying, "I'm having a breakdown. I'm just glad it's not this way everywhere."

I had left my room and came back to find these two maids in the bathroom handling my razor and looking through my things. I had to have a security guard outside my door. I couldn't leave my room. I couldn't go down to the lobby. I couldn't go outside. I couldn't go anywhere. And I wasn't used to this. I was used to twenty years of walking around left alone and unnoticed. It was rough. The fans all wanted to touch you; they'd pull at your hair, too, and I don't like being touched.

By the second and third time we toured there, we started having to play about a week of consecutive shows at the same venue to five thousand people a night. There would be big crowds of people waiting for us outside the hotels—all the time. I'd go outside, and I'd say, "I want you all to stand here. I'm gonna go out and walk around for half an hour, but I will come back, and I'll sign all the autographs. Nobody follow me—you all stay right here." They'd listen at first, but after the second or third day, they'd stop listening. One time they all jumped on me and started pulling my hair. I broke away and got in the door, and the hotel told us, "We don't want you back here anymore, because this is out of control. We can't deal with this." We went to another hotel, and they said, "Don't come down to the lobby." But I did, and the fans stormed the glass! They broke the entire front glass doors down and all charged into the lobby. I had to run out of there. I saw them coming through, jumped in the elevator, and got away. We had to get a hotel that had a fence around it, with guards outside and everything. There was no way of going anywhere.

Joey didn't really leave his room, either. CJ would go sit in the lobby and talk to the local girls there. He couldn't speak the language, but he didn't care. I can't do that. I'd try for a few minutes, and think to myself, "What am I doing?" It's too tiring talking to foreigners. It's a slow process, and you can't have meaningful conversation.

I was having a breakdown. I had the promoter fly Eddie Vedder down so I'd have a friend with me. I said, "My friend Eddie Vedder is really interested in playing down here." He really had no interest in playing down there at all, but I said, "I think it's a great idea for you to fly him down so he can see how great South America is." The promoter said, "He will, he'll come down?" I said, "Yeah," and they flew him down the next day. The promoter paid. They put him up in the room next to me with connecting doors. We'd sit there and play the Strat-O-Matic baseball game all day long. But I would go downstairs two times a day to sign stuff for the fans. There was a fence around the whole hotel, so they would pass stuff over the fence, and I would sign.

It would be funny playing the shows there, though, because we didn't know what the hits were. We'd play a song and feel it out, and realize, "Wow, I guess this was a big hit here." But almost every other song the audience would sing along. For "The KKK Took My Baby Away," the entire audience sang along. We must have had airplay there. The promoters own the record companies, and they own the radio. A monopoly; and it was good for us. We got paid a lot to play there, and they flew us in first class too.

The fans would sing along with songs, like "Psycho Therapy" and our version of "Have You Ever Seen the Rain?" We'd play a song and it would get such a huge response that I always had to wonder if that was a hit there and I just didn't know it. Almost the whole crowd was guys; there were some girls in the back. They were really good people who spoke very little English. When we played the five-thousand-seat place, there were these seats at the side of the hall that were more expensive. The kids on the floor would make fun of them up there, saying they weren't real Ramones fans, and that the Ramones were a band for the working class. They did it in a kind of football chant, like you hear in England.

We'd go on to play fifty-thousand-seat stadiums there; and in May of 1994, only two years after its release, South America gave us our first gold record, for the *Mondo Bizarro* album. About a month later, we received our first certified gold record in the United States, for the greatest hits compilation *RamonesMania*, released in 1988.

It was really nice, but at the same time, I had to think that we deserved that everywhere; like in the States. We'd play for fifty thousand people somewhere else, then come back and play clubs for one thousand people. It was the same when we first went to London and played the Roundhouse or the Hammersmith for two or three thousand people, then we'd come back here and try to get a show at Toad's Place in New Haven for five hundred people or play CBGB's. There was no one to blame, that's just how it went.

But near the end, our albums had long since gotten weak, and I was very protective of how we were looking and how the fans would see us. Some of us looked worse than others, and I was trying to avoid any clear shots of the band. On the last studio album, ¡Adios Amigos!, we went for the cover photo shoot, and I told them that we were keeping our backs to the cameras. Then I said that I wanted a firing squad shot that showed us against a wall being executed. But I wanted the name of the record company on the backs of the firing squad that was shooting us. They wouldn't go for that. But I did get the concession that our faces would not be used on the back cover, only inside. The label people were always trying to get one over on us. I learned from End of the Century. Never turn your back—except on the album cover when you might be looking too old.

These were the things that I had to worry about as we moved toward the end. Any band will tell you, if they're being honest, that rock and roll is a young man's game and that when you're in it too long, there are penalties. The last thing I wanted to be was like an aging athlete; Nolan Ryan, playing past his prime. You get up there, and you might be hitting .300, but you're not what you were. The songs, too, were a little tired. There is only so much creativity in the human soul.

Since 1977, for some reason, I'd had my eye on California as a place to retire. I didn't even know it, really, but I would mention it, jokingly, to interviewers. What's not to like? The weather is great all the time, you can drive around, which I love, and the food is tremendous, with so many great restaurants.

By the early nineties I had reached my financial goal. I had a million dollars saved, and since then I'd even started to surpass it. I was in the lobby of a hotel in May 1995. The place was empty except for me and a fan, a guy who had often followed us around on the road. I was watching ESPN, and a thought crossed my mind that had been bouncing around for a while. I was now certain of retirement, and that the Ramones were done. I'd mentioned it to this fan as an aside.

Once I told somebody that I was going to do it, it was done. I thought more about it that night, when we played and later in the hotel. I ran it by Linda, and we started planning. I felt that we could do one more album, which would be ¡Adios Amigos!, one of our better ones, then play everywhere the fans wanted us to play, and that would be it. I talked to the band about it, and there was no resistance. None. We just knew it was time, kind of like a clock striking. There we were, with our rock and roll hearts ready to go on to whatever else we were destined to do. For Joey, it was to DJ at New York parties and do some solo project. For me, it was to do nothing but my hobbies, although I was still interested in getting into the movie business.

In fact, after we'd retired, I specifically wanted to direct a remake of the 1971 exploitation film *Werewolves on Wheels*. I'd even planned to cast an actor named John Enos as the lead; he was Traci Lords's boyfriend at the time. I would casually bring up the idea to some friends in the industry from time to time, but in the end, as fate would have it, I never got the chance to seriously pursue it.

Even if we had gotten along, it was time to call it a day. We were treading water, and there was no point anymore. I thought we were becoming dinosaurs, which is why you see the dinosaurs on the cover of *¡Adios Amigos!*

There was no firm date on retirement, which is why we kept saying that each tour was our last in 1995 and 1996. Our final tour was as long as we wanted it to be. And at that point, it became more enjoyable. The pressures had subsided, and I began to savor those last months. Everyone in the band got along better; even Joey and I had kind of an unspoken agreement that we could get along in some way.

Throughout our career, it was sometimes hard to put happiness together with the experience of being in the Ramones, except for that time onstage. There was always pressure to put out a good record without compromising in any way. And at the same time, we had to listen to a label's ideas and be a little cooperative. Then there were the personnel issues, making sure that people in the band were not drug addicts and that they kept playing well. There were always lots of arguments, which was stressful. And it was sometimes hard to have fun at the job when someone would show up at practice drunk or stoned. I was always satisfied that we were the best, but it was a real job.

After the decision to retire, though, I knew that people were looking to us to be good for that last stretch, and there was so much appreciation—everywhere we went. Everyone in the band was straight, and I could relish each show. There was a peace, and it felt good. And the fans were still getting a great show.

The organizers of Lollapalooza had ignored us for years, ever since that tour began in 1991. I really didn't care. Our fans liked clubs, intimate gatherings, not the amphitheaters that Lollapalooza played. But when word got out that we were ready

to do one last swing through America, Lollapalooza called. I did this for Joey, who really thought it would be a good thing.

Marc Geiger, the guy who assembled the bands for Lollapalooza, came up to me at one point during the tour and said, "I got you on Lollapalooza." I said, "I don't give a shit; my career is over," and I walked away. I had no idea who ran the whole thing, and I couldn't have cared less. And then this guy was trying to take credit for having us on it, like he did me a big favor. He wasn't there when we really could have used it, in the early nineties. Besides, it was really Soundgarden who lobbied to get us on the tour.

This was how the business was run, on who could take credit for the coolness factor. The Ramones were cool no matter who wanted to take credit later.

We were on almost every show of Lollapalooza '96, and played as if we were headlining. In my mind, we were, because the people who were into us were not Soundgarden fans. They came to see us. We played before Metallica and Soundgarden and did a forty-five-minute set. I felt like I wasn't even working. I flew home after every show, since we'd usually play every two days.

ABOVE: Eddie Vedder, Chris Cornell, and Johnny backstage at Lollapalooza. Used courtesy JRA LLC photo archives. All rights reserved.

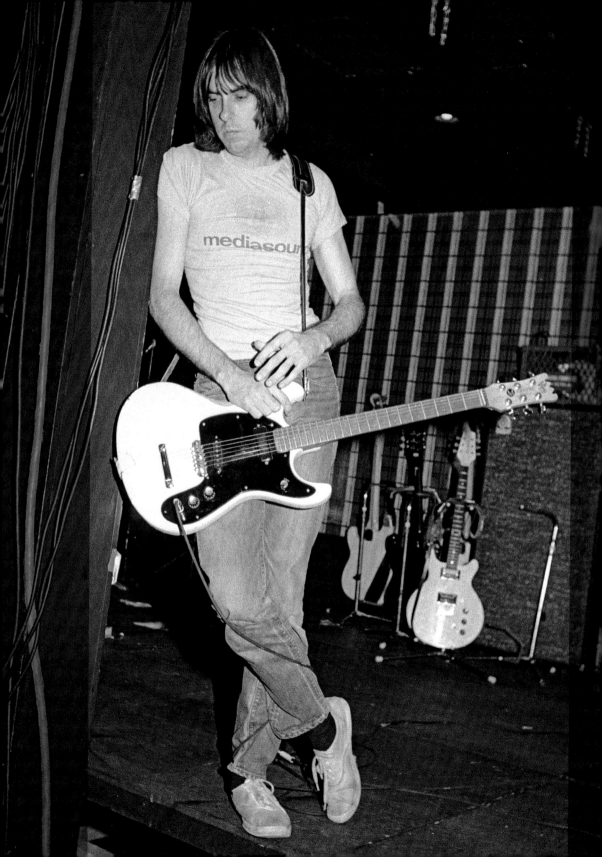

CHAPTER 7

THEN ONE DAY IT ENDED. THE MUSIC WAS OVER, REALLY, IN MY HEAD. I HAD ENOUGH MONEY, THE DOLLAR FIGURE THAT I HAD BEEN FOCUSED ON FOR SOME TIME.

We had accomplished what we needed to. Joey was getting more and more tired. But still, never at any point did I see a band in the nineties and think, "These guys are better than us." And we played with good bands.

I knew that someday it had to end. What a great job, what great fans we had. I mean, there are people who really have to work for a living. They work in coal mines; they sweep streets; they collect garbage. Being in a band was taxing on the mind because of all the travel, and there were certain pressures, but it was nothing like *real* work that most people do. I'm sure baseball is more grueling. I was very lucky.

Bands are fooling themselves if they think they're as good after playing together for fifteen years as they were three or four years in. It just doesn't work like that. We were no exception. Maybe there should be a mandatory retirement age for rock and roll. I probably would have been past it, at forty-seven, when I quit. But hey, I lied about my age when we started, making myself three years younger since I was actually the oldest guy in the band.

The last show was the end, and I knew it. I had no reservations about ending things. I had a life to look forward to. On August 6, 1996, the day of the last Ramones show, at the Hollywood Palace, I had blocked out the significance and the finality of it all. One thing I noted that was pretty cool is that the Palace was the same place that Dean Martin had mocked the Stones when he was guest hosting the variety show *The Hollywood Palace* in 1964. I always liked being on stages where my favorite bands had played. This time, though, was really the Last Time.

As for the show, it was number 2,263, the last performance we would ever make. I was happy to retire and be done with it, since I had planned this for many years. I had banked so much money and lived cheap. Funny thing, though, is that I could live on the royalty checks and barely even touch the core amount I had saved. We got so popular after we retired. I never expected it.

The show was being filmed, which was a hassle, and I was getting the pressure to come up with guests to go onstage and play with us. It was all on my head. We had special guests like Eddie Vedder and the guys from Rancid. I had to take care of all that.

That was how it ended, pretty much the same as it always was, with me doing a lot of the things.

After playing the last chords of the Dave Clark Five's "Any Way You Want It" and walking out of the Palace that night, it hadn't really hit me that it was over. I wasn't quite sure that we weren't going to play again. I said nothing to the other guys; I just walked out. It was the way I lived my life. I tried not to feel anything. The anger that I had used to carry myself through was now becoming a finely tuned dispassion for anything but relaxing. I was ready for the rest of my life, whatever that was going to be. Of course, I was really feeling loss of some sort. I just didn't want to admit it.

Before the last show, we had gotten a big offer to go to South America again and play some farewell gigs there, right away, just a week or two after the Palace. We had just played Lollapalooza for six weeks and had a chance to make more money than we did on that entire tour, for just three shows in South America. Joey said he was tired, but I told him, "Look, I just did Lollapalooza for you." The other guys wanted to do it, but Joey wanted to wait. So I said, "Hey, this is it. If we don't do that, I don't want to play anymore." He should have known that I don't give in on something like that. We do it when they ask us to do it, and that's that. If we weren't going to do that, I was done.

I got so tired of hearing from everybody about how fragile Joey was. It was always, "Oh, just be nice to him, he's tired." But it was used as an excuse for his behavior. Whenever we'd take time off, instead of resting, Joey would be out there doing all of these other projects. We'd get back on the road, and he'd immediately complain about how tired he was, and I'd think, "We just had a month off! Why didn't you relax?" I wasn't the only one in the band that noticed this, either. We all did.

He wasn't resting anyway, and he wasn't going to get himself in shape sitting around doing nothing unless he started doing some sort of exercise. You get home from a trip and three or four days later you're rested. We weren't working like those periods in the seventies when we had been playing constantly. Later on we weren't working that hard. But he tortured me every day, saying, "I've got to think of myself"; and here I am thinking about the band.

I rarely had any contact with Joey after we broke up; two or three times maybe, at the most. We would talk when there was a business issue and I wanted his opinion, or when I needed to tell him about something that I was doing for the Ramones, but that was it. When we did the *Anthology* in-store on Broadway in New York in 1998, I asked him how he was feeling. This was after I found out he had lymphoma, which eventually killed him. "I'm doing great," he said to me. "Why?" I gave up.

There were times on the road when a month would go by and I wouldn't say a word to him. It was pointless. If I got off the stage and said, "Wow, it was a good show tonight," he'd say something like, "Well, I thought it sucked!" And I'd think, "Why did I even bother saying a word? Why do I say anything?" This whole situation has always kind of weighed on me when I think of our fans. I don't think the fans want to hear that their favorite band disliked each other. They want to believe that you're friends, but that's only a public image.

In my mind, though, there was always that chance that we would get back together in the studio, maybe to do a song for a compilation or to add to a re-release.

OPPOSITE: Johnny, Joey, and Dee Dee, August 4, 1979.

Photo by Stephanie Chernikowski. Under license to JRA LLC. All rights reserved.

"IF THE RAMONES HAD NEVER EXISTED AND CAME OUT RIGHT NOW, WE WOULD STILL BLOW PEOPLE AWAY. THE RAMONES WERE NEVER SUPPLANTED BY ANYONE."

I kept a guitar around to play, just in case something came up. I would never join another band; I knew that. There was no way to top the Ramones.

In my head, it was never officially over until Joey died in April 2001. There was no more Ramones without Joey. He was irreplaceable, no matter what a pain he was. He was actually the most difficult person I have ever dealt with in my life. I didn't want him to die though. I wouldn't have wanted to play without him no matter how I felt about him; we were in it together. He never quit. We broke up and he died. That was the official end of the Ramones. I wasn't going to play without him. So when it happened, I was sad about the end of the Ramones. I thought I wouldn't care and I did, so it was weird. I guess all of a sudden, I did miss him. But he made an impact through his life, so he's still among us.

Dee Dee's death in June 2002 was a real blow to me, more than Joey's maybe, because Dee Dee and I had remained friends in some ways. I had no idea that he was going to die; I didn't even know that he was still using drugs. I had seen him on Hollywood Boulevard a few days before he passed away. Here's the most influential punk rock bassist of all time, and he died on us like that. He could be a problem, but I was really thrown by his death.

He was the craziest person there is in terms of eccentricities. It doesn't get any crazier. If you were to meet Dee Dee right now, he'd be the craziest person you're ever going to meet.

People have asked me, "What makes a punk?" About five years after we'd retired, I was driving in Los Angeles, and somebody called out to me, "Hey, you're driving a Cadillac. How's that? How are you a punk if you're driving a Cadillac?" I said, "What the fuck are you talking about? I wrote the book on punk. I decide what's punk. If I'm driving a Cadillac, it's punk." And the kid accepted that. So what determines a punk? Dee Dee was a punk. He had the look, he was a great songwriter, and he was the most influential punk rock bassist of all time. No one else even comes close.

But those last swings, Lollapalooza, the shows we did in New York at Coney Island High before that as a kind of farewell to New York—those were so satisfying. I really got to see what we meant to people. They told me how influential we were, and I got asked, "How does it feel to be a legend?" I didn't know quite how to answer that, and the first time I was a little shocked. Then it became a joke later on. I'd get a phone call at home, and a reporter would tell me I was a legend, and I'd hang up and tell Linda, "Hey, watch it. You're talking to a legend." Or I would answer the phone and say, "Legend here." I knew they were just treating Johnny Ramone like that; it wasn't really me.

So I came to realize the impact we'd actually made much later. We were in our own little world so much that I'd never thought about it at all until the nineties, when all these other bands started telling me what an influence we were all the time. To me, the greatest American band—besides the Ramones—is the Doors. They're my favorite American band, but I don't know how many other groups they really influenced. So when I realize that we might have been a bigger influence on more bands than anyone, it's surreal. There are even people wearing Ramones shirts now that don't even know what we were about or what we sounded like. I don't care, though. I'm just glad that our name is still out there after all these years.

We've been told that we changed music, that we created an entire genre, and that we mobilized kids and challenged them to get guitars and play their own music. It feels really weird to have people tell me that I influenced their lives or music. But I understand kids for going out and starting a band after seeing us. I would have done the same thing if I'd been in the audience in 1977.

If the Ramones had never existed and came out right now, we would still blow people away. The Ramones were never supplanted by anyone. Even when bands like Pearl Jam and Soundgarden hit it big, I never noticed a lack of support for us, or that our fans were straying.

Looking at it now, maybe a little less connected because I'm sick and time has kind of dwindled for me, the most important part of the Ramones legacy was that when we got up on a stage, we were the best out there. Nobody came close.

CHAPTER 8

THE WHOLE CANCER THING, IT'S BAD AND SOMETIMES CONFUSING. I WAS NEVER SICK; I WAS NEVER VULNERABLE.

I rarely even had colds. I had hay fever when I was growing up, and that was it.

All my life, I had this 100 percent belief that I would never get sick. If someone came over with the flu, I would still sit around with them. When I was a kid, I smoked pot with this friend of mine who had hepatitis. I just figured, "I can't get this."

Can you imagine how I felt when I started feeling funny in 1997? I was scared. I was having a hard time urinating. I knew that was part of what prostate cancer was, but I had no idea what it all meant. I never had cancer in my family. I was thinking it could be an enlarged prostate. It was getting bad, though, where Linda and I would have to leave places because I couldn't piss and was uncomfortable. Cancer? Not really. I had never even considered a prostate check when I was at the doctor. I wasn't even fifty years old.

So I went to a nutritionist in Santa Monica, which was weird for me in the first place since I wasn't the kind of guy who would go to something like that. I told him my symptoms, and he told me that we'd deal with it and he'd fix me up through nutrition.

He had me eating vegetables, whatever I could eat. I don't like to eat a lot of things that are super healthy, like broccoli or cauliflower. So I would eat Chinese food with peppers and corn and things like that, and vegetable soup and juices.

I was always skeptical about it all, but I stuck with this guy for a few months. Nothing got better. He had me eating better foods, which was fine anyway. But after a couple of months, he suggested I get my PSA checked because nothing was helping. I didn't even have a primary care physician, although I had a Blue Cross plan that I'd bought when I was in the Ramones, sort of a self-employed thing.

So I got my blood tested, and my PSA was high, a twelve. Really high. That's when the nutritionist got out of the game; he really panicked. By now, this stuff was weighing on me, in addition to the discomfort. I went in for a biopsy with a urologist in Culver City. I asked the doctor if this was going to hurt, and he told me, "A little bit."

It hurt like hell. I mean, it was unbelievable.

They stick this thing up your penis, way up there, and take twelve snips. It took ten minutes, and tears were running out of my eyes from the pain. I could barely walk out of there.

Then the results came back, and it was bad, again. I had a nine on a scale of ten for the Gleason score. They didn't know if the cancer had spread from my prostate into other parts of my body.

They told me I had to do something, and fast. I mean, I'd had some emergencies in my life, like the appendectomy in 1974 and the head injury in 1983, and this was urgent, but there was at least a little time to think about it. Now that was emotionally painful—to come to a decision that will affect whether you live or die and the quality of your remaining time. I decided to go with radiation rather than surgery. I wanted something with the least side effects.

First, I called a cancer center in Seattle, but there was a six-month wait, so Linda and I got on a plane to Oklahoma City, and on July 24, 1998, I had radiation treatment at the Cancer Treatment Centers of America. I was there for three days. They put me out for the treatment and stuck catheters in me. They also told me that the cancer had been in my prostate for five years at that point.

The doctors I went to during this whole thing, anywhere, knew who I was, because it would always come up. They would ask what I did, and I would say "retired" or "unemployed." That usually led to some discussion. I was in the Ramones. That wasn't such a big deal when you have prostate cancer.

The treatment was over, and I was told that I had a 65 percent chance of living five more years. I went home to continue some radiation treatment at UCLA. I went four days a week for six weeks. It was fine. I drove myself; Linda would come with me. And when it was over, I felt confident that they had fixed the problem. The symptoms eased up, but they would never completely go away.

They also told me that this was an aggressive cancer and that the younger you were, the more aggressive some of them can be. There was never a time when cancer left my mind, and I never felt that I had it completely beat, but I did think at some points that I would make it. I would read things about prostate cancer, but Linda didn't like me to because I would get so upset. Everything I read somehow told me that what I had was really bad. The books would describe the worst-case scenario, and that would be mine.

My life was simple after the radiation, and things got a little better. We had dinners out with friends, went to the movies, and took trips to Las Vegas and Florida. I went to the gym regularly; I had a trainer, and I lifted weights. And I would go to the doctor regularly so they could check to see if the cancer had come back. They checked my prostate and did a bone scan annually, because that's where the cancer can easily spread.

In addition to my hobbies, collecting autographed photos, vintage movie posters, and baseball memorabilia, I also had some more Ramones stuff to do. I oversaw the tribute album, *We're a Happy Family*, and put together *Loud, Fast Ramones: Their Toughest Hits* during that time.

Still, the cancer clawed at me physically and in my mind. I kept changing doctors in order to find one that I liked and finally got one, on January 27, 2003, at Cedars-Sinai Medical Center: Dr. David Agus, research director of the Louis Warschaw Prostate Cancer Center. And Dr. Agus is the man to whom I entrusted my life.

At the end of 2002, my PSA started going up. I was having more trouble with the urination. But I felt fine. That's the hard thing about this sickness. You feel OK, but you have it. This time, though, when the doctor told me my PSA was up, I sensed somehow that there was more. Then I began to understand, through our conversations, that it had spread. I went in to the doctor one day and told him I had a cough. "That's because you have spots on your lungs," he said. So that's how I found out that things had gotten really bad. Five years. I'd almost made it. I still didn't feel that I was going to die. I knew that my time was limited, but I didn't know what that limit was.

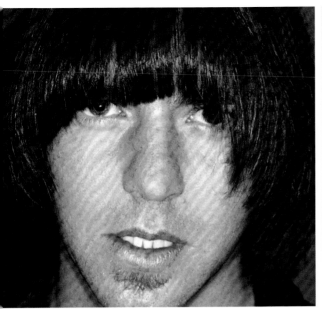

Shortly after I met Dr. Agus, he put me on chemotherapy right away; the disease was out of control. I have talked to Dr. Agus every other day for the past year. He has been the best doctor I could have hoped for. People tell me to get another opinion sometimes, but now I don't even bother. I have too much confidence in him; he's too smart. I need so many little things, like a blood transfusion, and I get advice from everybody I know, but I'm not listening to them. If Dr. Agus can't save me, nobody can. I liked him right away, and that was that.

It was funny. The Red Hot Chili Peppers and Pearl Jam did separate benefits for Cedars-Sinai prostate cancer research, and I took Dr. Agus to both of them. He had never been to a concert before. He sat on the side of the stage, and he was scared. He says he's a nerd, and I tell him, "I don't think you're a nerd. I find you interesting."

When I had the chemo, I was sick, and I couldn't tell if it was from the chemo or the cancer. My hair fell out three weeks after the first treatment, in two days, in huge clumps. I mean, I know it's just hair, but it was devastating.

I got a wig made, a professionally made wig that cost four thousand dollars. I wore it one time, to the premiere of Rob Zombie's movie, and I felt ridiculous. No one could tell, but I felt that someone might be able to. I gave it to Eddie Vedder; he likes that stuff. One night he was hanging out with Theo Epstein, the general manager of the Boston Red Sox. He called me the next day and said, "I was drunk last night and took photos with the wig on."

ABOVE: Eddie Vedder and Theo Epstein wearing the wig.

He sent them to me and they were hysterical. Eddie and Theo, drinking and wearing the wig. The photos were worth the four grand.

Psychologically it's hard. I didn't even know I could get sick. I always figured I could beat anything that happened, and it was devastating when I found out how serious and advanced my illness was. I never thought the cancer was causing me physical pain, except that sometimes I'd experience what felt like a bruise on the left side of my ass. I don't know what that was, but Dr. Agus said I had significant cancer that had spread to my bones, and much of the feeling I described was probably caused by that. I've had seven different kinds of chemo treatments. They were rough, and the side effects were brutal. I put up with this torture, and sometimes I wake up and don't even know if I feel like living. I never know what's in store for me.

There are questions that my doctor will not answer. But I do know that there are symptoms that will never go away. My instinct was to not talk about it at all. I get so sick sometimes, though, that people can tell, and I have to answer to that. So it doesn't matter anymore. And much of the time, no one is recognizing me. It beats you down so that you don't feel the same about yourself. I do have good days. Some are better than others.

In June 2004, I developed an infection and nearly died. I wasn't doing well for a few days there in late May, and I don't even remember driving to the hospital. I was feeling badly. The next thing I knew, I woke up and it was June 8. I was tied to a bed, and I had tubes coming out of me. I had been unconscious the whole time, for a week. What had happened was that they had done something to me, some treatment, and it had poisoned my whole body. They told my wife that I was going to die, that I had less than a 1 percent chance of living.

There was a chalkboard on the wall when I woke up that day, and Linda and Lisa Marie Presley were sitting there with me. I tried to write something on the chalkboard, but all that came out was squiggles; I couldn't keep my hand straight. It was very frustrating. Then they gave me a board with letters, and I would point to individual letters to make words, but I also couldn't point straight; I was pointing between the letters.

That's when it became public knowledge that I had cancer, and I wasn't even in the hospital for cancer at that point. Mark was the one who had blabbed, to RollingStone.com, that I was dying and on my deathbed. That really wasn't his business.

Ramones guitarist Johnny Ramone is in a Los Angeles hospital battling prostate cancer, according to his longtime bandmate, drummer Marky Ramone. "Johnny's been a champ in confronting this, but at this point I think the chances are slim," says Marky... "I've been getting so much email from people and from papers and magazines wanting to know what was up I had to take it upon myself to say something, because eventually John won't be in any condition to say or do anything," Marky says.

Here I was in recovery, out of intensive care, and Mark takes it upon himself to tell the world my "chances are slim." The phone never stopped ringing. Linda and I were furious, so we decided it would be best to authorize Dr. Agus to explain my condition to Kurt Loder, from MTV, who'd called the hospital.

Johnny Ramone is not dying, according to his doctor.

The Ramones guitarist, who has been living with prostate cancer for the past several years, was recently admitted to Cedars-Sinai Medical Center in Los Angeles with what his physician, Dr. David Agus, told MTV News was a "complication from the cancer. But he got through it, and he's now on a new, experimental therapy. He's fighting courageously, and I think he will be going home in the near term."

"He's not dying," Linda said on Wednesday afternoon (June 16). "He was okay for years, and he's fine now. He's in the hospital, but he's not in ICU. And I think he may be leaving by tomorrow."

I called Mark after I got out of the hospital and told him, "You really have to control yourself, control what you're saying. You're desperate for attention." He said he was dealing with rumors, but there were no rumors. No one knew until Mark broke the news to get his name in the press. He'd do anything to get his name in the press. He was always like that.

Mark and I always went back and forth, and it's not my fault, it's his. He has all these bad ideas and I tell him that we can't just do things for a quick buck. We have to make sure the Ramones are well represented; we have to do what's best for the Ramones. And when we do something Ramones-related, I'm in charge, not him. He just doesn't get it. I'm all for making money, but we have to have standards. I've had to stop him from doing Ramones things all the time, especially since the band retired. I try to tell him that it's not like I'm doing anything against him, but he resents it, so he spends a lot of time trying to badmouth me, every chance he gets. He did the same thing to Joey for a long time too. Then after Joey died, Mark practically went on a press junket about it. He's always looking for any attention he can get.

As I said before, the whole cancer thing is confusing. I've always been into health and things, taking vitamins. I went to the gym, had a trainer. I lifted weights. I only gained twenty pounds over the years the band was playing, from 150 to 170.

I don't care to be a role model for illness. I just know that I had to tell people that I was sick; so many people already knew. If a situation ever came up where I could help other people with this, I would do it.

As far as medicine goes, I will try anything that does not interfere with what Dr. Agus says to do, so I even tried a healer. Kirk Hammett from Metallica had recommended him, and it didn't make any sense, but I tried it. I would call him up, and he would say to lie down and relax for fifteen minutes. While I'd do that, he would do something at his house, like look at a photo of me. It's wacky, and it didn't work.

It's interesting that I have never felt that I was going to die until this last time. I've known that my time is limited, but I had nothing definite. If this happens again, I want them to just let me die. I won't go through that again.

Of course, now I know. We all have time limits, and mine came a little early.

By the time you are reading this book, I might not be here. But I've had a great life no matter how it turns out now. I think that when I lost my job back in 1974, it was God looking after me. All of a sudden I got into a band, and I had success. I've been very lucky and very fortunate in life. I owe everything I have to the fans. I've had the best wife, Linda, that I could ever hope to find, and I've had such great friends, who really care and would do anything they could for me.

On Johnny's plot at Hollywood Forever, a cemetery off Santa Monica Boulevard, the same one where Dee Dee was buried in 2002, stands an eight-foot-tall bronze statue of Johnny. "It's me from the guitar up" is how Johnny described it a month before he died.

Carved in the base of the monument is a simple statement, dictated by Johnny: *"If a man can tell if he's been successful in his life by having great friends, then I have been very successful."*

JOHNNY WAS A DEAR FRIEND. HE WAS GROUCHY, HE WAS LOYAL, kindhearted, soft on the inside, set in his ways, and well . . . grouchy :) We were similar, which is why we got along so well. He took a paternal role in my life, and I respected and loved him dearly. Johnny handpicked certain people to be in his orbit, and I feel fortunate to have been one of them.

The day Johnny died, in his chair at his Los Angeles home, was one of the most incredulous, fantastic, and macabre experiences of my life. He waited until his orbit of loved ones was surrounding him, and then he let go . . . Linda (his wife), Eddie Vedder, John Frusciante, Vincent Gallo, Steve Jones, Rob Zombie, Pete Yorn, and my husband and I all gathered around him for hours, telling stories into the night, saying our farewells, laughing, crying, and sitting around him—even sitting around him while watching the coverage on the news that he had passed away. It was incredibly profound and comforting. It was a punk rock and rock and roll version of the movie *The Big Chill*.

He was taken away and cremated the next morning. It was very much like an Irish wake and exactly the way Johnny would have wanted it to be. It is also how he liked things to be in life—surrounded by who and what he liked—and it was punk rock. I will never forget that, and I will never forget him . . . He was a legend, a good friend, and well . . . he was grouchy :)

—*Lisa Marie Presley*

OPPOSITE TOP: Johnny and Lisa Marie, 2001.

OPPOSITE BOTTOM: On January 14, 2005, the eight-foot-tall bronze Johnny Ramone Memorial Statue was unveiled by Johnny's wife and companion of over two decades, Linda Ramone. (From left to right) Eddie Vedder, Rob Zombie, Nicolas Cage, Linda Ramone, John Frusciante, Vincent Gallo, Pete Yorn, Tommy Ramone, CJ Ramone, Lisa Marie Presley and husband Michael Lockwood, and Seymour Stein. Used courtesy JRA LLC photo archives. All rights reserved.

2191 shows

week AT·A·GLANCE
1996

For
planning,
appointments
and memoranda
on a weekly
basis

© 1994 Keith Clark
Made in USA

MONDAY, FEBRUARY 26

THURSDAY, FEBRUARY 29
Played New York, N.Y.
Academy
Sold out
Att - 1550
Pay - 15,516

TUESDAY, FEBRUARY 27
Played New York, N.Y.
Coney Island High
* Eddie Comes to show
Att - 450   Sold out
Pay - 10,000

FRIDAY, MARCH 1

WEDNESDAY, FEBRUARY 28
Played New York, N.Y.
Coney Island High
Att - 350   Sold out
Pay - 10,000

SATURDAY, MARCH 2

SUNDAY, MARCH 3

MONDAY
16   June 16—22, 1975

TUESDAY
17

WEDNESDAY
18

THURSDAY
19

FRIDAY
20   Played C.B.G.B's
          With Talking Heads

SAT.   Played
21   C.B.G.B's

SUN.   Played
22   C.B.G.B's

June 23—29, 1975

Played For Sire
Received Offer

Played For Blue Sky

Played For Arista   WE

TH

SAT.
28

AUGUST

Album—114

...y PLAYED
Golden Bear
...ington Beach, Cal.

...y PLAYED
Golden Bear
...ington Beach, Cal.F.

...SDAY
Fest n Fair
...ington Beach, Cal.

...DAY
Went to
Disneyland

August 8—14, 1977

MONDAY 8

TUESDAY 9 Filmed Don Kirschner Rock Concert

WEDNESDAY 10 Played L.A. Whiskey w/ Mink + dookies

Att.– 900 2 shows
Pay – 2800
THURSDAY 11 Back to N.Y.

FRIDAY 12

SAT. 13   **SUN. 14**

August 15—21, 1977

MONDAY 15

TUESDAY 16 Elvis Dies

WEDNESDAY 17

THURSDAY 18

FRIDAY 19

SAT. 20 Start Recording   **SUN. 21**

December 26, 1977—January 1, 1978

MONDAY 26 Day OFF

TUESDAY 27 Day OFF

WEDNESDAY 28 Played Birmingham, Eng. Top Rank

Att.– 1700
THURSDAY 29 Played Stoke on Tren /Victoria Hall

Att. – 1050
FRIDAY 30 Played Aylesbury, Eng Friars

Att. – 1250 Sold out
SAT. 31 Played London Rainbow Theatre w/Rezillos, Generation X
SUN. 1 January, 1978 New Year's Day Played Lond Rainbow Theat

Att.– 2962 sold out   Att.– 2800

Job –146

DECEMBER 1974

MONDAY 30

TUESDAY 31 Went to hospital

WEDNESDAY 1 JANUARY 1975   NEW YEA

...es

Started Album
with Phil Spector

...ed

4 fri

5 sat Pop Dies At 12:00 Noon Flew to N.Y.

6 sun Went to Florida

...m —
...t the Hassle
...e of Rock + Ball
SUNDAY 28 Movies – Last Detail

...vies
...as Chain
...w Massacre of a window Cleand
...ttles
...e New
SUNDAY 10 Movies – Confession

...num –
...oey Boyles
...W.W.
Uncle
...awish Delights
SUNDAY 12 MOTHER'S DAY Movies– Sugarland Express

SATURDAY 4 Album – N.Y. Dolls Too Much too Soon
SUNDAY 5 Movies– Freaks – + Fellini: Satyricon

SATURDAY 16 Played – PERFORMANCE
SUNDAY 17 Played – C.B.G.B.

SATURDAY 18 Movies– Exorcist
SUNDAY 19 The Sting

1976   JUNE

MONDAY 7 Album 193 in Billboard

MONDAY, MARCH 11 Played Sao Paulo, Brazil Olympia

Att– 3700

TUESDAY, MARCH 12 Played Sao Paulo, Brazil Olympia

Att– 3914

WEDNESDAY, MARCH 13 Played Sao Paulo, Brazil Olympia *Eddie at show sold ot

Att– 4513

THURSDAY, MARCH 14

FRIDAY, MARCH 15

SATURDAY, MARCH 16 Played Buenos Aires, Argen River Plate Stadium Att.– 43,000 *Eddie At show
SUNDAY, MARCH 17 ST. PATRICK'S DAY

Job

Bought Guitar

WEDNESDAY 23

WEDNESDAY 14

Movies – Chinatown

THURSDAY 24

THURSDAY 15

... Kenny's (cathouse?)
Slouch - Punk + Riganey Bye

FRIDAY 25

FRIDAY 16   Ramones Play at
                     CBGB

SATURDAY 26   SUNDAY 27   Rehearsed

SATURDAY 17   Ramones
                       Play at
                       CBGB

SUNDAY 18

SATURDAY 24   Played CBGB   SUNDAY   Play
                                                          25   CBGB
                                                                   Movies – Bo...
                                                                             B:

1976

1976   MARCH

MONDAY 29

TUESDAY 30

WEDNESDAY 31

THURSDAY APRIL
                      1 Played C.B.G.B's
with Milk + Cookies

APRIL   197...

Played 'G.B.G.B's   FRIDA...
       with Milk + Cookies 2
collected #950

Played C.B.G.B's   SATURDA...
       with Milk + Cookies 3
collected #1200

MOVIES –   SUNDA...
       Taxi Driver 4

NOTES

DECEMBER 1973

MONDAY 31   Concert – Academy of Music
                      Kiss, Teenage Lust,
Stooges , Blue Oyster Cult

TUESDAY 1   JANUARY 1974   NEW YEAR'S DAY

WEDNESDAY 2

THURSDAY 3

FRIDAY 4

SATURDAY 5   SUNDAY 6

JANUARY 1974

MONDAY 7

TUESDAY 8

WEDNESDAY 9

THURSDAY 10

FRIDAY 11

SATURDAY 12   Got Color TV   SUNDAY 13
Went to Country
Flaming Youth + Teenage...

MONDAY 8   September 8—14, 1975

TUESDAY 9

WEDNESDAY 10

THURSDAY 11

FRIDAY 12   Played At Performance
                      Studio
                      with Blondie

SAT.   Played at   SUN.
12   ...

September 15—21, 1975
Yom Kippur

RECORDED JUDY's
                     PUNK
Upstate

MOVIES –   SAT.

ALBUM-BY-ALBUM ASSESSMENT BY
JOHNNY RAMONE

RAMONES
RELEASED: April 23, 1976, Sire Records;
REISSUED: June 19, 2001, Warner
Archives / Rhino

Produced by Craig Leon; recorded at
Plaza Sound, Radio City Music Hall,
New York City. On Rhino reissue,
executive producer Johnny Ramone.

Blitzkrieg Bop • Beat on the Brat • Judy Is a Punk
• I Wanna Be Your Boyfriend • Chain Saw • Now I
Wanna Sniff Some Glue • I Don't Wanna Go Down
to the Basement • Loudmouth • Havana Affair •
Listen to My Heart • 53rd & 3rd • Let's Dance •
I Don't Wanna Walk Around with You • Today
Your Love, Tomorrow the World

Bonus tracks on Rhino release: I Wanna Be Your
Boyfriend (demo) • Judy Is a Punk (demo) •
I Don't Care (demo) • I Can't Be (demo) • Now I
Wanna Sniff Some Glue (demo) • I Don't Wanna
Be Learned/I Don't Wanna Be Tamed (demo)
• You Should Never Have Opened That Door
(demo) • Blitzkrieg Bop (single version)

RAMONES | Grade: A

After each take, the engineers would ask if I wanted to hear it back, and I'd ask them how it sounded.

"It sounded good."

So I just said, "OK, let's keep going." I didn't need to hear it back. I wanted to move on.

We did all our tracks in two days at Radio City Music Hall. We were rushing because I knew we would have to pay back the money that we'd bought the new equipment with, so the less time it took, the cheaper it was. We got this done for sixty-five hundred dollars, which was cheap even then.

It slowed down when it came time for Joey to do the vocals. He recorded them once, then he did them all over again. He said he had a cold the first time. I think we wasted some money there, but he may have really been sick. It was winter.

They put the guitar in one channel, which I thought was weird. I didn't like it, but others were OK with it, so I let it go. The mix for the first album has the guitar in one channel and the bass in the other. So, if you listen to the album and mute your left speaker, you'll just hear guitar without bass. If you mute the right, you'll just hear the bass without guitar.

I had these brand-new Marshall amps that had been bought for us after we'd signed the contract, but I got into the studio and didn't know what to do. I had the amps and some brand-new guitars and a new playing field. This album was vastly different from the fourteen-song demo we had recorded at some studio on Long Island, where we just plugged in and played the set. They put me in a different room to record the guitar, which I thought was strange but found out later was normal. The songs had all been written fairly quickly when we'd gotten together to rehearse from the beginning.

"Blitzkrieg Bop" was our "Saturday Night," you know, that song by the Bay City Rollers. We had to have some kind of chant just like they did. Dee Dee's work there. We'd heard the Bay City Rollers doing "Saturday Night." And we thought that was our competition. So we had to come up with a song that had a chant because they had one too. It's funny, I originally wanted to be a ballplayer, and now they play "Blitzkrieg Bop" at a lot of the parks. They play it at Yankee Stadium all the time.

To date, the Ramones' 1976 self-titled debut remains the best-selling album in the band's entire catalog, worldwide, surpassed in sales only by the greatest hits compilation RamonesMania.

LEAVE HOME | Grade: A

We recorded the first two albums in the order we wrote them. All of those songs were already written by the time we signed to Sire. We wanted the second album to be a little different from the first, which is why we didn't really mix up the songs between the two. If we had, our first two albums would have sounded very similar. By recording and releasing them this way, there was a slight progression in the songs, and our ability, from one album to the next. You could hear our development. Some of these we couldn't have done on the first album. But we were better players, faster and more skilled at this point. We used the normal stereo mix, with the guitar and bass in both channels this time, rather than the split-channel mix that our first album had.

We wrote a lot of the music for this album in my apartment in Forest Hills, all four of us sitting around and me with an unplugged electric guitar, playing into a cassette deck. We kept playing a lot of these songs in our live show right to the end.

A lot of people listen to music and, though they may not be conscious of it, its influence comes out when they write their own songs. Well, when I listened to songs, I couldn't play them back even if I wanted to, so they always came out different. I wrote the song "Carbona Not Glue" after listening to an Eddie Cochran album. But I don't think you can hear that in there. The Carbona company made us pull the song from the album. They didn't want us singing about sniffing the stuff, but I thought the song was funny. I sniffed Carbona a couple of times. It was worse than glue. We replaced the song with "Sheena Is a Punk Rocker" on the American repressings and "Babysitter" on the others. So because of this, there were three different vinyl versions of *Leave Home* in print between the United States and Europe.

ROCKET TO RUSSIA | Grade: A+

This was the best Ramones album, with the classics on it. The band had reached its peak both in the studio and live. This one has one great song after another, most of them written between our first and second albums. It has just the right balance of slow songs, ballads, and rockers. I loved "Here Today, Gone Tomorrow." "I Don't Care" was actually one of our first songs, and we played that before we ever recorded anything. From here on, we played pretty much this whole album live. The band was getting along great. I loved the back cover. John Holmstrom did the artwork and I worked with him on some of the ideas, doing the drawing with a military theme and playing into my strong anti-Communist stance in a cartoonish manner.

LEAVE HOME
RELEASED: February 1977, Sire Records
REISSUED: June 19, 2001, Warner
Archives / Rhino

Produced by Tony Bongiovi and
Tommy Erdelyi; recorded at Sundragon,
New York. On Rhino reissue, executive
producer Johnny Ramone.

Glad to See You Go • Gimme Gimme Shock
Treatment • I Remember You • Oh Oh I Love He
So • Carbona Not Glue • Suzy Is a Headbanger •
Pinhead • Now I Wanna Be a Good Boy • Swallow
My Pride • What's Your Game • California Sun •
Commando • You're Gonna Kill That Girl • You
Should Never Have Opened That Door

Bonus tracks on Rhino reissue: Babysitte
• Recorded live at the Roxy, Hollywood, CA
8/12/76): Loudmouth • Beat on the Brat
Blitzkrieg Bop • I Remember You • Glad to Se
You Go • Chain Saw • 53rd & 3rd • I Wanna B
Your Boyfriend • Havana Affair • Listen to M
Heart • California Sun • Judy Is a Punk • I Don'
Wanna Walk Around with You • Today You
Love, Tomorrow the World • Now I Wanna Sni
Some Glue • Let's Dance

ROCKET TO RUSSIA
RELEASED: October 28, 1977, Sire Record
REISSUED: June 21, 2001, Warner
Archives / Rhino

Produced by Tony Bongiovi and Tomm
Erdelyi; recorded at Media Sound,
New York. On Rhino reissue, executive
producer Johnny Ramone.

I wanted drawings to represent all of the songs on the inside sleeve, and I had the concept for the back cover too. I asked for a pinhead riding a rocket over a cartoon map of the world. There were specific details I wanted on the map too, like the Empire State Building for New York, and the Capitol building for Washington, D.C.

As of the time of this writing, the original artwork is on display at the Rock and Roll Hall of Fame and Museum in Cleveland, Ohio.

ROAD TO RUIN | Grade: A

The production on this is the best of all of them, and there are so many good songs on it. "I Wanted Everything," "Bad Brain," "Go Mental"—they're all great songs, so great that I can't narrow it down to my favorite. Joey came to rehearsal with "I Wanna Be Sedated" and played it for us on his one-string guitar. He had it all together, the verse, the chorus, the arrangement.

By this time, I didn't have a guitar at home, so I would show up fifteen minutes early to rehearsal and start working on something, and sometimes I'd work on new material in a dressing room somewhere. I'd come up with a rhythm and then find a chord combination I liked. It's possible that I wrote the same song a few times, which, when it was pointed out, I would concede. I played acoustic guitar on a few songs here. Ed Stasium did the fills on some of those more country-sounding songs, like "Questioningly," a song I didn't like. Ed was into the Eagles and stuff, so that worked. The recording process got a little longer, and the price went up, from the sixty-five hundred dollars on our first one to about thirty thousand dollars at this point. This was the last of the great Ramones albums until *Too Tough to Die.*

ROAD TO RUIN

RELEASED: September 22, 1978, Sire Records
REISSUED: June 19, 2001, Warner Archives / Rhino

Produced by T. Erdelyi and Ed Stasium; recorded at Media Sound, New York. On Rhino reissue, executive producer Johnny Ramone.

I Just Want to Have Something to Do • I Wanted Everything • Don't Come Close • I Don't Want You • Needles and Pins • I'm Against It • I Wanna Be Sedated • Go Mental • Questioningly • She's the One • Bad Brain • It's a Long Way Back

Bonus tracks on Rhino reissue: I Want You Around (Ed Stasium version) • Rock 'n' Roll High School (Ed Stasium version) • Blitzkrieg Bop-Teenage Lobotomy-California Sun-Pinhead-She's the One (live) • Come Back, She Cried A.K.A. I Walk Out (demo) • Yea, Yea (demo)

END OF THE CENTURY | Grade: B

These were really good songs that were marred by the production of Phil Spector, who, ironically, was supposed to deliver the Ramones' first hit record. It's interesting that the songs were this strong, because it was really the first time we had to write an entire album from scratch. We had the luxury of having songs already written on the first few records. Some of the songs here came out muddy, like on "Rock 'n' Roll Radio," which Joey wrote and is a great song. I can't hear my guitar on it. Same with "I'm Affected." The record took four to six weeks to do, and I left just as it started because my father died.

Nothing is bad on this record, and I'd like to hear it with different production. There are other high points, like "Chinese Rock," which I didn't want to do at first because it was about dope. Then I realized that it was just a good song after the Heartbreakers did it on *L.A.M.F.* "Let's Go" is a song that Dee Dee and I wrote about the Vietnam War, another song about war. I enjoyed handling that subject in a heroic way, rather than a protest way.

The low point was "Baby, I Love You," which the band didn't even play on. It was the band's worst moment ever. The only extra guitar stuff is some of the overdubs done by Ed Stasium, and I didn't have much input on that this time.

END OF THE CENTURY
RELEASED: January 30, 1980, Sire Records
REISSUED: August 20, 2002, Warner
Archives / Rhino

Produced by Phil Spector. Recorded
at Gold Star Studios, Los Angeles;
Devonshire Sound Studios, Salty Dog
Studios, and Original Sound Studios.
On Rhino reissue, executive producer
Johnny Ramone.

Do You Remember Rock 'n' Roll Radio? • I'm
Affected • Danny Says • Chinese Rock • The
Return of Jackie and Judy • Let's Go • Baby, I
Love You • I Can't Make It on Time • This Ain't
Havana • Rock 'n' Roll High School • All the Way
• High Risk Insurance

Bonus tracks on Rhino reissue: I Want You
Around (soundtrack version) • Danny Says
(demo) • I'm Affected (demo) • Please Don't
Leave (demo) • All the Way (demo) • Do You
Remember Rock 'n' Roll Radio? (demo)

Alternate shot—with leather jackets on—from *End of the Century* album cover photo shoot. Photo © Mick Rock, used under license to JRA, LLC. All rights reserved.

PLEASANT DREAMS
RELEASED: July 15, 1981, Sire Records
REISSUED: August 20, 2002, Warner
Archives / Rhino

Produced by Graham Gouldman;
recorded at Media Sound, New York
City. On Rhino reissue, executive
producer Johnny Ramone.

We Want the Airwaves • All's Quiet on the Eastern
Front • The KKK Took My Baby Away • Don't Go
• You Sound Like You're Sick • It's Not My Place
(In the 9 to 5 World) • She's a Sensation • 7-11 •
You Didn't Mean Anything to Me • Come On Now
• This Business Is Killing Me • Sitting in My Room

Bonus tracks on Rhino reissue: Touring (1981
version) • I Can't Get You out of My Mind • Chop
Suey (alternate version) • Sleeping Troubles
(demo) • Kicks to Try (demo) • I'm Not an
Answer (demo) • Stares in This Town (demo)

PLEASANT DREAMS | Grade: B-

One of the first things that happened when we got to the studio was that the producer, Graham Gouldman, said, "What's that humming noise?" Well, it was my guitar, just like it always sounded. He told me to fix that, and so I knew that things weren't going to go well. I mean, he was from 10cc. On top of that, nobody in the band was speaking, and I didn't write any songs with Dee Dee, so it has no real punk songs on it; it's too light. There are keyboards in there, and I don't have a problem with that when they're called for. The single was "We Want the Airwaves," and I didn't like that song. My favorite on here is "The KKK Took My Baby Away," which we did live for a long time. The Linda issue was big by this time too, and when Gouldman wanted to go to England to mix it, Joey went with him for whatever reason. He took Linda too, which I wasn't pleased about. Also, on this record we all went into the studio at the same time. It was awkward, since we weren't talking to each other. This is not one of my favorites, to say the least.

SUBTERRANEAN JUNGLE | Grade: B

It was kind of a good time. Dee Dee and I were working together. Linda had just moved out of Joey's place on Ninth Street and Third Avenue, and we had gotten an apartment together on Twenty-second Street.

My personal life was starting to come together. We were having trouble with Mark because his drinking problem was really bad. So we did "Time Has Come Today" with a different drummer, Billy Rogers, from Walter Lure's band. We did three covers, and we shouldn't have, but I was happy with the guitar sound on it. We were going in the right direction with this record. We did a cover of "Indian Giver," and the producers didn't like it, which I think was because they had worked on the original, by the 1910 Fruitgum Company. I was watching the Brewers-Cardinals World Series when we were recording it.

TOO TOUGH TO DIE | Grade: A-

All of a sudden, we all got along and stopped worrying about making a hit record—as a result, this is a really good album. Tommy and Ed produced it, and it has a great guitar sound. All the songs are solid. Joey wasn't at the rehearsals for the album, though. Dee Dee had a lot of input on this, which helped make it such a good album, and he sang "Wart Hog." We wrote several of the songs together, too, which made a big difference.

I'd have to lobby for songs. Joey had voted against "Psycho-therapy" on *Subterranean Jungle*, and this time he was voting against "Wart Hog." There are all these songs that are now classic Ramones songs that he voted against. And if I hadn't lobbied for them, they wouldn't have been on the albums.

At this point in our career, when the record company wanted to hear some songs that we were going to use, I would just tell them to listen to the last five albums, and that's what these were going to sound like, but different. That was it. They never really asked me much more, and we delivered. This was our best record of the eighties.

TOO TOUGH TO DIE
RELEASED: October 1, 1984, Sire Records
REISSUED: August 20, 2002, Warner
Archives / Rhino

Produced by T. Erdelyi and Ed Stasium;
recorded at Media Sound, New York
City. On Rhino reissue, executive
producer Johnny Ramone.

Mama's Boy • I'm Not Afraid of Life • Too Tough
to Die • Durango 95 • Wart Hog • Danger Zone •
Chasing the Night • Howling at the Moon (Sha-
La-La) • Daytime Dilemma (Dangers of Love)
• Planet Earth 1988 • Humankind • Endless
Vacation • No Go

Bonus tracks on Rhino reissue: Street Fighting
Man • Smash You • Howling at the Moon (Sha-
La-La) (demo) • Planet Earth 1988 (Dee Dee
vocal version) • Daytime Dilemma (Dangers
of Love) (demo) • Endless Vacation (demo) •
Danger Zone (Dee Dee vocal version) • Out of
Here • Mama's Boy (demo) • I'm Not an Answer
• Too Tough to Die (Dee Dee vocal version) • No
Go (demo)

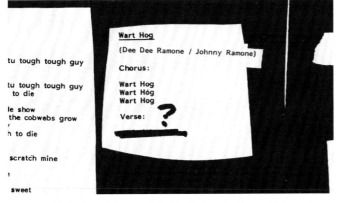

Excerpt from inside sleeve of the original 1984 Sire LP release *Too Tough to Die*. Verses to "Wart Hog" were left off due to controversy with the lyrics.

ANIMAL BOY
RELEASED: May 19, 1986, Sire / Warner
Brothers

Produced by Jean Beauvoir; recorded at
Intergalactic Studios, New York.

Somebody Put Something in My Drink • Animal
Boy • Love Kills • Apeman Hop • She Belongs
to Me • Crummy Stuff • My Brain Is Hanging
Upside Down (Bonzo Goes to Bitburg) • Mental
Hell • Eat That Rat • Freak of Nature • Hair of
the Dog • Something to Believe In

ANIMAL BOY | Grade: B-

To John. Best wishes
Nancy Reagan

This would have worked if the production had been better, but the guitar doesn't even sound like me. I liked the songs, though; they were all brand-new. Dee Dee and I wrote the music to "Freak of Nature" while they were changing reels in the studio. This is also the album where Dee Dee and Joey wrote the song about Reagan's visit to Germany, but I wouldn't let them put it out with the original title, "Bonzo Goes to Bitburg." It appears as "My Brain Is Hanging Upside Down." They couldn't talk about my favorite president like that. So we agreed to use another title.

Dee Dee was always leaning to the right. I don't know why he wrote that. Maybe he believed that it could be popular in Europe. I sure wasn't happy. I didn't want politics in the songs anyway. When I was in the Ramones, I never wanted it to be about politics. There's video out there that has me saying that we aren't political, and that was true. Joey was a far left liberal, a hippie, and he would speak out sometimes and it would make me cringe. He even did some of that "We Are the World" stuff. I spoke out once in a while. One time I told a college newspaper in Oregon that Ronald Reagan was all right but he wasn't conservative enough. I did it to get a reaction, just to irritate people.

Like on a lot of later albums, we ended up doing maybe four songs off the whole thing during the tour because the material just didn't measure up to our other stuff. The producer on this, Jean Beauvoir, was selected by the label, not us.

HALFWAY TO SANITY | Grade: B-

This was recorded during a stressful time in the Ramones. Joey and Richie made it hard for Daniel Rey, who was producing the album. They kept wanting to change things and remix songs. The best of them are "I Wanna Live," "Weasel Face," "Bop 'til You Drop," and "Garden of Serenity." Dee Dee and I wrote "Weasel Face" about a guy who had a real weasel face. He came to all our gigs in the South; he followed us around. I think he was from Mississippi. The tracks on this one aren't the best. I always had a problem bringing songs into

To Johnny
all the
very
best!

Paul
McCartney
OR
(RAMON!!)

OPPOSITE: Autographed photo of Nancy Reagan personalized to Johnny, from the private collection of Johnny Ramone. Used courtesy JRA LLC.
ABOVE: Autographed photo of Paul McCartney, personalized to Johnny, and acknowledging the influence of Sir McCartney's early alias "Ramon" and its historical relevance to the Ramones. From the private collection of Johnny Ramone. Used Courtesy JRA LLC.

HALFWAY TO SANITY
RELEASED: September 15, 1987, Sire /
Warner Brothers

Produced by the Ramones and Daniel
Rey; recorded at Intergalactic Studios,
New York City.

I Wanna Live • Bop 'til You Drop • Garden of
Serenity • Weasel Face • Go Lil' Camaro Go •
I Know Better Now • Death of Me • I Lost My
Mind • A Real Cool Time • I'm Not Jesus • Bye
Bye Baby • Worm Man

the band unless I was sure they were going to be very good. I was very selective because I didn't want to embarrass myself. The other guys brought in things that sucked, but they acted like they were great. We shot the album cover in New York City's Chinatown, keeping it dark. It had to be pretty good not to make us look old, and it was getting harder and harder.

Also, Dee Dee was credited as bass player here but didn't play on the album. Daniel played his parts. Debbie Harry did guest backing vocals on "Go Lil' Camaro Go."

BRAIN DRAIN | Grade: C

One of my least favorite albums, but it has a couple of bright spots, like "I Believe in Miracles" and "Punishment Fits the Crime." Bill Laswell's production is too dense; he had me record the guitars on five or six tracks. So the album took too much time, and there were too many Joey songs on it, which always took more time. "Miracles" was the song we kept in our live repertoire for a while, and "Pet Sematary," which we wrote for the Stephen King movie, was also a live song for a while. That came out OK. We also covered "Palisades Park," which may have been my idea, but it came out lousy. This was the last album Dee Dee was credited on, but again, he didn't play on it.

Autographed photo of Stephen King (personalized to Johnny), from the private collection of Johnny Ramone. Used courtesy JRA LLC.

MONDO BIZARRO | Grade: C

The songs are the weak spot on this album. Dee Dee's "Main Man" and "Strength to Endure" are the best ones, and we kept doing them live to the end. But we needed more Dee Dee songs on it. I didn't write anything on this record; it was two from Mark and some Dee Dee and Joey. CJ was in the band, but his material wasn't up to par yet. I liked working with Ed Stasium again, but he was producing things a little differently now, piecing things together and using multiple tracks on the drums, and so it was more time-consuming. It also cut into the spontaneity of the recording. We did a Doors cover, "Take It As It Comes." It was my idea, which nobody liked at first. But Joey did a great job on the vocals, and it shows, because the song works. I didn't like the lyrics on "Censorshit." They were stupid. Joey wrote this song about Tipper Gore, and then he goes and votes for Bill Clinton. I don't think he even knew that Tipper Gore was the vice president's wife. I liked the song, though. The band was doing well by this time, making more money than ever, playing festivals and bigger shows. I had my eye on hitting twenty years together when we recorded this. It was a goal I had, and we were getting close.

ACID EATERS | Grade: B-

This is hit-and-miss, but overall I think we did a good job. A lot of these songs were done with studio work, arrangements, and tricks, which was really different for us. "Out of Time" was one of those. We practiced it, and it didn't sound quite right. But once we added some things, it came out fine. We never could have done this album early in our career, because the songs would have had to be adapted to a strict Ramones style, like "California Sun."

Here, we experimented to mixed success. Joey did a great job on "Out of Time." CJ sang some of these and also did well, like on "The Shape of Things to Come." "Somebody to Love" came out OK, but it was a hard song to sing. I never liked the Jefferson Airplane, but I guess Grace Slick was pretty good. Traci Lords did backing vocals on that one too. On "My Back Pages," we just skipped over the Byrds' and Dylan's versions and did it Ramones style. "Surf City" fell short because we didn't do it in the right key. Joey never rehearsed it with us, so it didn't come out right.

One of the problems was that as we undertook this, we were getting all kinds of suggestions from everybody, and it was getting to be a pain in the ass. I mean, "She's Not There" by the Zombies? Some of the most logical songs don't work when you're doing this. It's always hard to pick covers, and after all those years it was still hard to tell.

MONDO BIZARRO
RELEASED: September 1, 1992,
Radioactive Records

Produced by Ed Stasium; recorded at
the Magic Shop, NYC, and Baby Monster
Studio, NYC

Censorshit • The Job That Ate My Brain •
Poison Heart • Anxiety • Strength to Endure
• It's Gonna Be Alright • Take It As It Comes •
Main Man • Tomorrow She Goes Away • I Won't
Let It Happen • Cabbies on Crack • Heidi Is a
Headcase • Touring

ACID EATERS
RELEASED: January 4, 1994, Radioactive
Records

Produced by Scott Hackwith; recorded
at Baby Monster Studio, New York City.

(Left) Johnny with Traci Lords. Photo by Bill Mullen. (Right) Johnny with actor Michael Berryman on the set of the Ramones music video "Substitute." Used courtesy JRA LLC photo archives. All rights reserved.

Pete Townshend came in to do backing vocals on "Substitute." He is one of the greats and one of my guitar heroes, but he was late. I stuck around for a half hour waiting for him. After a while, I started wondering if he was going to show up at all, and everyone was getting excited about talking to him. That was not how I wanted to meet him, so I left to go watch the Yankee game.

¡ADIOS AMIGOS! | Grade: B+

¡ADIOS AMIGOS!
RELEASED: July 18, 1995, Radioactive
Records

Produced by Daniel Rey; recorded at
Baby Monster Studio, New York City.

I Don't Want to Grow Up • Makin Monsters
for My Friends • It's Not for Me to Know • The
Crusher • Life's a Gas • Take the Pain Away •
I Love You • Cretin Family • Have a Nice Day
• Scattergun • Got Alot to Say • She Talks to
Rainbows • Born to Die in Berlin

Hidden track on U.S. CD edition: Spider Man

This album has perhaps the best of all the guitar sounds I ever got. Daniel Rey produced it, and he knew that the Ramones were a guitar group. He also played the leads on here. Some of our albums would have three or four really strong songs, and then the rest would be pretty weak. But on this one, even the lesser stuff is decent. My favorite is "The Crusher." I love "Scattergun." We did a cover of Tom Waits's "I Don't Want to Grow Up." I had never heard the song before; I just showed up one day, and CJ played it for me, and I said, "Sure." I didn't really write anything on this, but I played well and got to do anything I wanted. I got CJ to sing four songs; he had a good voice for some of these songs. On "Makin Monsters for My Friends," the demo from Dee Dee had Dee Dee singing, and it worked well when CJ sang it; he had a whiny voice, and it sounded great.

The front cover is of dinosaurs, which is what we felt like. When we showed up for the shoot for the back cover, I told them that we were going to face away from the camera. The label said that I had agreed to take pictures, and I did, but I'd never said that we would face the camera. I was very protective of how we looked at that point, and some of us looked worse than others. I was trying to avoid any clear shots of the band. So the back cover is just a photo of us with our backs to a firing squad. I had asked that they put the name of the record company on the backs of the firing squad executing us, and they wouldn't go with that. I figured they wouldn't. But I just wanted to get them to say yes to something, which was that we wouldn't show our faces. And I won on that point.

At Carmen Miranda's family gatherings

JoHNNY

HAVE A HAPPY
HEALTHY
(WATCH THAT BACK)
WEALTHY
&
WILD
CHRISTMAS
YES — ITS BEEN
A FUCKIN GREAT
YEAR
1990

Happy Holidays!

ABOVE: Handwritten Christmas card to Johnny from Joey, 1990. From the private collection of Johnny Ramone. Used Courtesy JRA LLC. All rights reserved.

BELOW: The Ramones ring in the new year at the legendary "It's Alive" show at the Rainbow Theatre, London, December 31, 1977. Photo by Danny Fields, under license to JRA LLC. All rights reserved.

Johnny

1st

Blitzkrieg Bop
Beat on the Brat
Judy is a Punk
Loudmouth
53 + 3rd
Havana Affair + Boyfriend

Leave Home

Gimme Gimme Shock Treatment
I Remember You
Commando
Glad to See you Go
Carbona not Glue
Pinhead — Oh Oh I Love Her So

Rocket to Russia

Rockaway Beach
Happy Family
Here today Gone Tomorrow
Sheena is A Punk Rocker
Teenage Lobotomy
Cretin Hop

Road to Ruin | Mental

Sedated
Something to Do
I wanted Everything
I'm Against it
I Don't want you

End of the Century

R + R Radio
Danny Says
I'm Affected
R + R High School

Pleasant Dreams

K.K.K.
You Sound Like You're Sick
She's Sensation
Eastern Front
Subterranean Jungle
~~Animal Boy~~ Outsider
Highest Trails
Psycho Therapy
Time Bomb

Handwritten notes by Johnny Ramone indicating his favorite tracks from each of the respective Ramones albums listed.

④ Mondo Bizzaro (Radioactive)

Censorship
Main ✓
Straight to Endam ✓
I wont Let it Happen ✓
Take it As it Comes ✓

⑥ Adios Amigos

✓ Scattergun
✓ I dont wanna Grow up
Making Monsters For my Friends
✓ Crusher
Lifes A Gas
(RAMONES)

② HALF WAY to SANity

I want to Live
Garden of serenity
I Lost my mind
Bop Till you Drop

③ BRAIN DRAIN

MiRACLes
Pet Semetary
Merry Christmas
Punishment Fits the Crime

⑤ ACID EATERS

My Back PAges
I cant Control myself
Journey
Out of Time / 7+7 is

① Live

Anyway You want it

Spiderman

① Animal Boy

Animal Boy
Love Kills.
Something to Believe in
Somebody Put Something in my Drink
I Dont wanna Live this Life

Too tough to die

Mama's Boy
Wart Hog
Howling At the moon
Daytime Dreams
Too Tough to Die

Johnny Ramone's
ALL-TIME TOP TEN

1 **Baseball**

2 **Rock and roll**

3 **Politics**

4 **Elvis**

5 **Horror films**

6 **Film**

7 **Rock films**

8 **Science fiction films**

9 **Reference books**

10 **Television**

1A: BEST BALLPLAYERS OF THE NINETIES

1. Greg Maddux
2. Roger Clemens
3. Barry Bonds
4. Ken Griffey Jr.
5. Mark McGwire
6. Jeff Bagwell
7. Mike Piazza
8. Craig Biggio
9. Tom Glavine
10. Sammy Sosa

1B: BEST BALLPLAYERS OF THE EIGHTIES

1. Rickey Henderson
2. Mike Schmidt
3. Cal Ripken
4. Wade Boggs
5. Ryne Sandberg
6. Andre Dawson
7. Robin Yount
8. Tim Raines
9. George Brett
10. Tony Gwynn

2A: TOP PUNK GROUPS

1. The Ramones
2. The Clash
3. The Sex Pistols
4. The Heartbreakers
5. The Dead Boys
6. The Damned
7. The Cramps
8. The Buzzcocks
9. The Dickies
10. Black Flag

2B: TOP GUITARISTS

1. Jimmy Page
2. Jeff Beck
3. Leslie West
4. Jimi Hendrix
5. Dick Dale

6. Ron Asheton
7. James Williamson
8. Johnny Thunders
9. Keith Richards
10. George Harrison

2C: TOP SINGERS

1. Elvis
2. Bing Crosby
3. Roy Orbison
4. Gene Pitney
5. The Everly Brothers
6. Ricky Nelson
7. Dean Martin
8. Frankie Laine
9. Dion
10. Jim Morrison

3A: FAVORITE REPUBLICANS

1. Ronald Reagan
2. Richard Nixon
3. Charlton Heston
4. Vincent Gallo
5. Ted Nugent
6. Rush Limbaugh
7. Sean Hannity
8. Arnold Schwarzenegger
9. Bob Barr
10. Tom DeLay

I've always been a Republican. From the 1960 election with Nixon against Kennedy. At that point, I was basically just sick of people sitting there going, "Oh, I like this guy. He's so good-looking." I'm thinking, "This is sick. They all like him because he's good-looking?" And I started rooting for Nixon just because people thought he wasn't good-looking. And then by the time Goldwater ran and he starts talking about bombing Vietnam, I said, "This sounds right to me." Then I started realizing where my political leanings really lay.

I remember doing an interview in 1979 for *CREEM* magazine with Lester Bangs and telling him that Ronald Reagan will be the next president. He was really mad that I liked Reagan, who was the greatest president of my lifetime. So I turned it around on him and asked to see his Commie card. In fact, ever after that, I would ask him for his card. I think he had one, really.

At the Rock and Roll Hall of Fame, when I made my acceptance speech, I said, "God Bless President Bush, and God Bless America." It was the counter to those speeches at the awards. That sure set them off. I'm glad I said it. It got every response I intended it to. This wasn't long after September 11th either. I was always so gung-ho American, I felt that was a real attack on me.

4A: FAVORITE ELVIS FILMS

1. *Loving You*
2. *Jailhouse Rock*
3. *King Creole*
4. *Viva Las Vegas*
5. *Follow That Dream*
6. *Kid Galahad*
7. *Love Me Tender*
8. *Kissin' Cousins*
9. *Elvis: That's the Way It Is*
10. *G.I. Blues*

4B: FAVORITE ELVIS BOOKS

1. *Last Train to Memphis*
2. *Careless Love*
3. *Elvis Up Close*
4. *Elvis Aaron Presley: Revelations from the Memphis Mafia*
5. *That's Alright, Elvis*
6. *Elvis: What Happened?*
7. *All About Elvis*
8. *The Elvis Encyclopedia*
9. *Down at the End of Lonely Street*
10. *The Elvis Atlas*

4C: FAVORITE ELVIS SONGS

1. "Don't Be Cruel"
2. "Can't Help Falling in Love"
3. "Baby Let's Play House"
4. "Viva Las Vegas"
5. "Are You Lonesome Tonight?"
6. "Don't"
7. "Trying to Get to You"
8. "It's Now or Never"
9. "(Marie's the Name) His Latest Flame"
10. "All Shook Up"

5A: FAVORITE HORROR FILMS

1. *The Bride of Frankenstein* (1935)
2. *The Invisible Man* (1933)
3. *The Texas Chain Saw Massacre* (1974)
4. *Night of the Living Dead* (1968)
5. *King Kong* (1933)
6. *Re-Animator* (1985)
7. *The Evil Dead* (1981)
8. *The Wolf Man* (1941)
9. *Freaks* (1932)
10. *Psycho* (1960)

6A: FAVORITE FILMS OF THE NINETIES

1. *Buffalo '66*
2. *L.A. Confidential*
3. *Private Parts*
4. *Ed Wood*
5. *The Silence of the Lambs*
6. *Goodfellas*
7. *Seven*
8. *Pulp Fiction*
9. *Wild at Heart*
10. *Bugsy*

7A: BEST ROCK FILMS

1. *The T.A.M.I. Show*
2. *The Girl Can't Help It*
3. *High School Confidential!*
4. *Monterey Pop*
5. *The Buddy Holly Story*
6. *Gimme Shelter*
7. *Help!*
8. *A Hard Day's Night*
9. *Rock 'n' Roll High School*
10. *That'll Be the Day*

8A: BEST SCI-FI FILMS

1. *The Thing* (1951)
2. *Invasion of the Body Snatchers* (1956)
3. *Forbidden Planet* (1956)
4. *The Day the Earth Stood Still* (1951)
5. *Them!* (1954)
6. *Planet of the Apes* (1968)
7. *The War of the Worlds* (1953)
8. *The Incredible Shrinking Man* (1957)
9. *Invaders from Mars* (1953)
10. *Dr. Cyclops* (1940)

9A: BEST FILM REFERENCE BOOKS

1. *The Psychotronic Encyclopedia of Film*
2. *The Psychotronic Video Guide*
3. *The Film Encyclopedia*
4. *The Motion Picture Guide*
5. *Hollywood Rock*
6. *Leonard Maltin's TV Movies and Video Guide*
7. *Disney A to Z*
8. *The Encyclopedia of Horror Movies* (P. Hardy)
9. *The Encyclopedia of Science Fiction Movies*
10. *Blood and Black Lace* (guide to Italian horror)

10A: FAVORITE TV SHOWS

1. *Chiller Theatre* (with Zacherley)
2. *The Twilight Zone* (1959)
3. *The Outer Limits* (1963)
4. *The Honeymooners*
5. *Amos 'n Andy*
6. *Baseball Tonight*
7. *I Dream of Jeannie*
8. *The Beverly Hillbillies*
9. *The Addams Family*
10. *The Many Loves of Dobie Gillis*

LIFE IN LOS ANGELES

Johnny with friend John Frusciante

Johnny and friend Vincent Gallo (posing with the infamous white Mosrite guitar used throughout the Ramones legendary career), in what would soon become the Disney-themed bedroom of Johnny's (then) new home in Los Angeles

Kirk Hammett and Johnny at his home in LA

Johnny and Linda with friends Kirk and Lani Hammett at the Rainbow in LA

Actor John Enos, Johnny Ramone, and Lux Interior

With friend Slim Jim Phantom (of the Stray Cats) in Johnny's '58 Fairlane

Johnny in the Elvis Room of his home in Los Angeles

Friend Chris Cornell visits Johnny's Elvis Room

With friend and producer Rick Rubin, said that the two best bands are the B and the Ramones

Johnny with friend Rosanna Arquette

th friend and director Tim Burton

With friends Sex Pistols' Steve Jones and X's Billy Zoom at Johnny's 50th birthday party

Johnny and Linda (row 1), with friends Jacqui and Peter Getty (row 2), on the Dinosaur ride at Walt Disney World

Lisa Marie Presley, Marilyn Manson and Rob Zombie, en in Los Angeles

Johnny, with friend Vincent Gallo, storing his equipment in the garage of his Los Angeles home following the Ramones last show

, Lisa Marie Presley, Linda, and Johnny boarding private the *Lisa Marie* for a visit to Graceland

"IF A MAN CAN TELL IF HE'S BEEN SUCCESSFUL IN HIS LIFE BY HAVING GREAT FRIENDS, THEN I HAVE BEEN VERY SUCCESSFUL."

Nurse Linda, Johnny (as Elvis), and Sailor Girl Rose McGowan, Halloween 2001. Photo by Andrew Durham.

with Keith Richards and Johnny Depp at a Pearl Jam/Rolling Stones show

Johnny blows out the candles on his 52nd birthday cake, with friend Rose McGowan (who baked the cake personally), and Nic Cage seen in the background celebrating at Johnny's Los Angeles home, 2000

Thanks to:

Tommy Ramone, Lisa Marie Presley, Kirk Hammett, Suzanne Cafiero, Robert Guinsler, David Cashion, Curt Krasik, Steve Miller, Christian Fuller, Henry Rollins, Heidi May, Alan Nevins, Mason Williams, JD King, Barbara Ramone Zampini, Sandy Linter, Bill Mullen, Richard Adler, Robert Roland, Richard Whitley, Stephanie Chernikowski, Chuck Pulin, Danny Fields, Mick Rock, Bob Gruen, Sarah Field, Jenny Lens, Dave Toussaint, David Burd, Ed Stasium, Monte Melnick, Rick Weinman, Kelli Poff, Nancy Baum, Duggal Photo Lab, Beatriz Pace, Don Terbush, Elaine Woodall, Bob Koszela, Andrew D. Gore, Andrew Durham, Kris Ahrend, Charles Comparato, Eleonora Monacella, Hal Willlner, Zeina Hamzeh, Bobby Robertson, Rhino Entertainment, Warner Music Group, Universal Music Group, Warner/Chappell Music, everyone at Abrams Books, and Ramones fans everywhere.

THE FIRST TIME I MET JOHNNY RAMONE I WAS A SIXTEEN-YEAR-OLD FAN. For most of my life, the Ramones have been a huge part of it. They defined something that truly spoke to me and had a rare ability to maintain that omnipresent voice and powerful presence in my life (and the lives of other like-minded individuals around the world) for decades. It was always something I could relate to, both sonically and visually, transcending from childhood to adulthood, and only growing stronger with the passage of time.

As history—not to mention the blood and sweat (you read it right—no tears) of Johnny's life, which are thoroughly soaked into the pages of this book—reveals, the one person who emphatically refused to allow that purity to be diluted, more than anyone, was Johnny Ramone.

He was the boss, the institu-
tion, the establishment. Johnny was
the commander, and he had to be; if
not, despite the incredible talents
of his fellow cofounding Ramones
(Dee Dee, Joey, and Tommy), things
would never have progressed or pre-
vailed as they did, and continue to.
Someone has to make the rules and
ensure people adhere to them. Tough
love isn't always appreciated, but it
can be a crucial ingredient in shaping
things to come. Some people thought
Johnny was mean or unfriendly, but
he wasn't. He was authoritative, and
understandably, people don't like
being told what they can—or can't—
do. He's said it before, and in retro-
spect, in the role I have since become

engrained on his behalf, I understand now more than ever that if Johnny wasn't the way he was, the Ramones would not have become who and what they are. The look, the sound, and the simplistic perfection are things Johnny fought for constantly, and strived to keep alive.

For years, growing up, even into my young adulthood, I would persistently argue, fight, and champion the Ramones to what I felt was a world of narrow-minded, criticizing skeptics. Sadly, it took the deaths of my heroes to make the world finally stand up and recognize the brilliance that was right in front of them all the time. In literary terms, I think the Ramones are like the Edgar Allen Poe of rock and roll. They were largely unappreciated by the masses during their lifetime, but after the fact will forever be an integral part of the fabric of pop culture. They are forces that will remain timeless and relevant to all, conscious of it or not, for eternity.

The last time I saw Johnny in person, just months before he passed away, he said that he wanted me to become more involved in things. He couldn't have paid me a bigger compliment. It meant the world to me, and still does. Since then, the faith Linda has put in me in managing Johnny's estate, and all of his interests in the Ramones, as well as that same faith that Barbara has put in me on Dee Dee's behalf, is truly an incredible honor. Just as people who *really* know me have said, I believe it was fate. Seeing things come to fruition through passion and sheer determination is a genuinely rich and rewarding experience on many levels, and having the privilege and pleasure of being so deeply involved with something that's meant so much to me for so long is truly surreal. Responsibility and a genuine care for everything surrounding it is no easy task, but nothing worth fighting for is. I understand now more then ever, particularly from the inside, why Johnny was the way he was.

It was a huge honor seeing this project through to completion for Johnny Ramone. I agonized over every detail to ensure it was true to his words, his persona, and character; and like Johnny, I will always remain relentless, and never give up.

— John Cafiero

MY HUSBAND AND MY BEST FRIEND FOR OVER TWENTY YEARS, Johnny Ramone, would always say to me, "Linda, I am unique, a legend, and always right." And we would always laugh about it.

Every morning at breakfast we would discuss everyone and everything over waffles and blueberries. If the waffle was not perfect, or a blueberry was off, he would give me that look that only he could give and say, "Why? What have I done wrong?" And again we would just laugh.

To be able to keep his legacy alive, something that was so important to Johnny, and being a president of Ramones Productions and JRA LLC (Johnny Ramone Army), is the most amazing thing for me that I can do for him.

I love and miss my husband and best friend, Johnny, every single day of my life.

The truth is, he was unique, he is a legend, and he will always be right.

Luv,
Linda Ramone

Ramones / Too Tough To Die

HOWLING AT THE MOON (Sha-La-La) • DAYTIME DREAMA (Dreams Of Love)
PLANET EARTH 1988 • HUMAN KIND • ENDLESS VACATION • NO GO

SIRE
CASSETTE
AR

   2